ZIMBABWE

THE BEAUTIFUL

ZIMBABWE

THE BEAUTIFUL

STRUIK PUBLISHERS
(a member of The Struik Publishing Group (Pty) Ltd)
80 McKenzie Street, Cape Town 8001

Reg. No.: 54/00965/07

First published in 1996

Managing editor: Annlerie van Rooyen
Editor: Glynne Williamson
Design and DTP: Peter Bosman
Cover design: Peter Bosman
Assistant designer: Lellyn Creamer
DTP map: John Loubser
Thumbnail maps: Darren MacGurk

Reproduction: cmyk prepress
Printing and binding: Tien Wah Press (Pte.) Ltd, Singapore

ISBN 1 86825 776 2

CONTENTS

THE LIE OF THE LAND

Z IMBABWE IS A LARGE, LANDLOCKED, always attractive and sometimes breathtakingly lovely country that occupies nearly 400 000 square kilometres (154 446 square miles) of south-central Africa's sunlit grasslands. Its northern border, shared with the Republic of Zambia, is demarcated by the Zambezi River, whose reaches embrace the awesome Victoria Falls and, farther downstream, the spacious waters of Kariba, among the world's biggest man-made lakes. Another renowned river, Kipling's great and grey-green Limpopo (though it is greater in legend than in fact) forms the country's southern frontier with South Africa. The other national neighbours are Botswana in the west and southwest, and the long, narrow and, until recently, strife-torn state of Mozambique in the east. Zimbabwe also has a tiny common border – it's just a few hundred metres long – with Namibia's distinctive Caprivi panhandle.

About a quarter of the country is covered by the Highveld, a broad swathe of upland plateau that runs diagonally across the region from the semi-arid fringes of the Kalahari northwestwards to the scenically magnificent Nyanga mountains. The Highveld ridge, on which Zimbabwe's capital city of Harare is situated, rises some 1 500 metres (4 921 feet) above sea level and is the country's principal watershed. Cutting through the Highveld is a remarkable geophysical feature known as the Great Dyke, 515 kilometres (320 miles) long and at its narrowest, an 11 kilometres (7 miles) wide fault, thought to be associated with the Great Rift Valley that runs from the eastern Mediterranean through East Africa to Lake Malawi. The Dyke's ancient rocks contain fabulous deposits of minerals – gold, chrome and nickel among them.

To either side of the central ridge, and accounting for a further two-fifths of Zimbabwe, is the so-called middleveld at an altitude of 600-1 200 metres (1 968-3 937 feet), which falls down to the narrow strip of the Zambezi valley on one side and, more gradually, to the hot, dry flatlands of the Kalahari basin and the southeastern Lowveld on the other. For sheer beauty, few regions of the continent can compare with the high mountain rampart that runs along Zimbabwe's eastern border, from the majestic Nyanga range down through the misty and remarkably lovely uplands of the Bvumba to the forested and flower-graced grandeur of the Chimanimani. Below the highlands are wide and luxuriant valleys that yield fine harvests of tea, coffee, fruit and much else.

Zimbabwe lies to the north of the Tropic of Capricorn but is nevertheless blessed with a temperate climate, the summer heat moderated by the altitude in all but the lowest lying areas. Weather patterns are generally uniform, predictable: bone-dry winters of warm, sunny days and chilly, often bitter nights when temperatures, especially on the Highveld, plunge below zero. June and July are the coldest months, but summer is the wet season. In good years huge, dark banks of cumulonimbus clouds begin massing from October to disgorge their rains between November and February. The thunderstorms, which invariably occur in the latter part of the day, are often of Olympian proportions. Average rainfall is much higher in the north and northeast – where Chipinge, for instance, receives a healthy 1 100 millimetres (43 inches) a year – than it is in the sandy, semi-arid spaces of the south and southeast.

Page 1: A passageway winds through the Great Enclosure of the ancient Shona-Karanga city of Great Zimbabwe.

Pages 2-3: The tops of long-dead forests rise above the placid waters of Lake Kariba.

Pages 4-5: Buffalo congregate at the water's edge on Kariba's Fothergill Island Safari Lodge.

Pages 6-7: The stratified and dramatically sculpted columns of the Chilojo Cliffs tower above the Runde River in the Lowveld's Gonarezhou National Park.

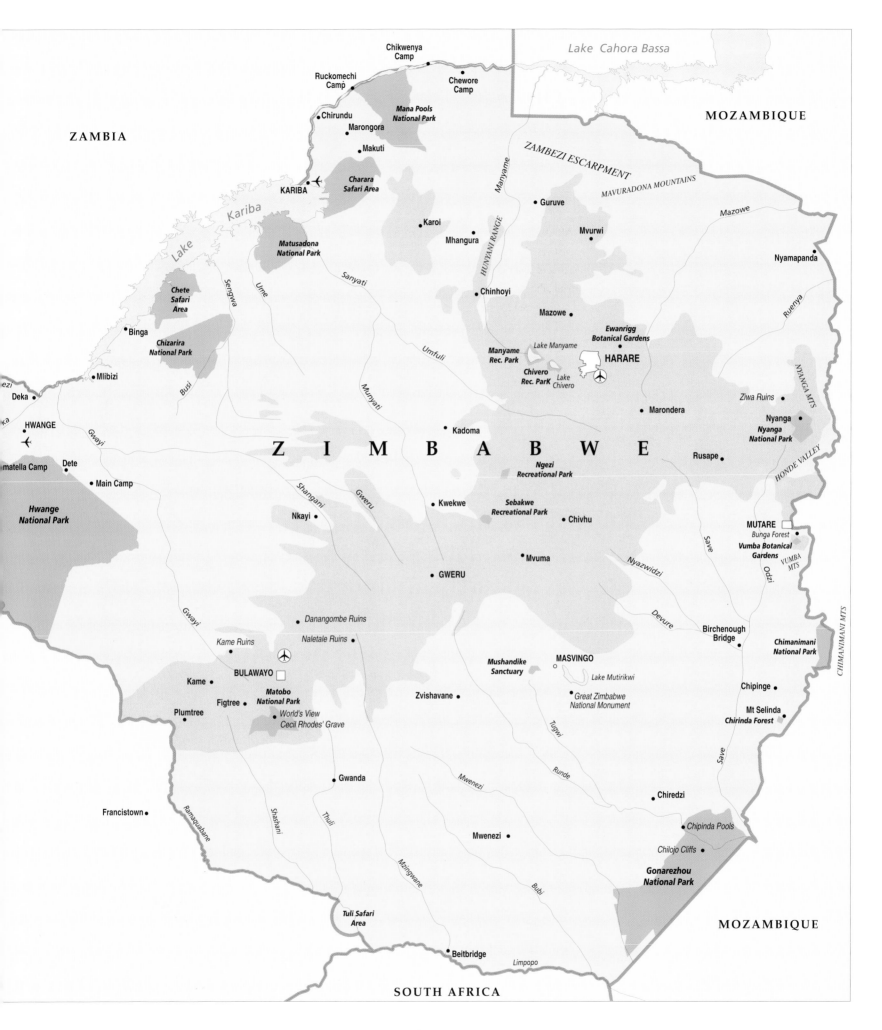

ZAMBIA

MOZAMBIQUE

Lake Cahora Bassa

Chikwenya Camp

Ruckomechi Camp

Chewore Camp

Chirundu

Marongora

Mana Pools National Park

Makuti

ZAMBEZI ESCARPMENT

MAVURADONA MOUNTAINS

KARIBA

Charara Safari Area

Guruve

Mvurwi

Mazowe

Nyamapanda

Lake

Kariba

Karoi

Mhangura

Matusadona National Park

Chinhoyi

Mazowe

Chete Safari Area

Sanyati

Ewanrigg Botanical Gardens

Binga

Umfuli

Lake Manyame

HARARE

Chizarira National Park

Sengwa

Ume

Manyame Rec. Park

Chivero Rec. ParK

Lake Chivero

Mlibizi

Busi

Munyati

Ziwa Ruins

Deka

Marondera

Nyanga

HWANGE

Gwayi

Kadoma

Rusape

Nyanga National Park

atella Camp

Dete

Ngezi Recreational Park

HONDE VALLEY

Main Camp

Shangani

Gweru

Kwekwe

Sebakwe Recreational Park

Chivhu

MUTARE

Hwange National Park

Nkayi

Bunga Forest

Vumba Botanical Gardens

Mvuma

VUMBA MTS

GWERU

Nyazwidzi

Danangombe Ruins

Devure

Birchenough Bridge

Kame Ruins

Chimanimani National Park

Naletale Ruins

Save

BULAWAYO

Mushandike Sanctuary

MASVINGO

Kame

Lake Mutirikwi

Chipinge

Figtree

Matobo National Park

Zvishavane

Great Zimbabwe National Monument

Mt Selinda

Plumtree

World's View Cecil Rhodes' Grave

Chirinda Forest

Gwanda

Tugwi

Runde

Chiredzi

Mwenezi

Francistown

Ramaquabane

Shashani

Thuli

Chipinda Pools

Chilojo Cliffs

Mwenezi

Mzingwane

Bubi

Gonarezhou National Park

Tuli Safari Area

MOZAMBIQUE

Beitbridge

Limpopo

SOUTH AFRICA

9

INTRODUCTION

A magnificently maned lion (opposite) surveys his kingdom in the Hwange National Park, Zimbabwe's foremost wildlife sanctuary. These big cats are just one of the park's 25 species of predator; others include the spotted hyaena and, occurring mainly in the north, the rarely seen leopard.

Two inventive youngsters show off their home-made toys (below), fashioned from wire and wooden oddments. Zimbabwe is home to around 13 million people, three-quarters of whom are under 30 years of age. The country has one of the world's highest population growth rates – a source of serious concern in a land where jobs are scarce and the potential for economic expansion limited.

THE ZAMBEZI RIVER, AFRICA'S fourth largest and arguably the continent's grandest and least spoilt watercourse, rises in the well-watered Lunda uplands of central Africa, gathering momentum as it flows south and then east to delineate the border between Zimbabwe and Zambia. It eventually enters Mozambique to discharge into the Indian Ocean, 3 540 kilometres (2 200 miles) from its headwaters. At one point, about a third of the way along its 2 740 kilometres-course (1 703 miles), the river plunges a hundred metres (328 feet) down into a maze of narrow, precipitous gorges in a series of gigantic cataracts, the tumultous descent producing a rising cloud of spray that can be seen about 40 kilometres (25 miles) away. The spreading mist also nurtures a rain forest of quite magical beauty.

These are the Victoria Falls, which the 19th-century Scottish missionary-explorer David Livingstone first sighted on 15 November 1855, on his epic journey (much of it by dugout canoe) across the African continent. The Falls, he wrote in his notebook, 'had never been seen before by European eyes. Scenes so lovely must have been gazed upon by angels in their flight'. On the following day he planted commemorative seeds of apricot and peach and, in an uncharacteristic exhibition of sentiment, carved his name on the trunk of a giant tree. The Kololo people of the upper Zambezi know the Falls as *Mosi-oa-Tunya*, which means 'the smoke that thunders'; the Ndebele call them *aManzi Thunquayo*, or 'the water that rises like smoke', and they are the country's pride, its grandest natural wonder and foremost among its many tourist attractions.

Indeed, Zimbabwe has a great deal to offer the visitor. Its wildlife heritage, encompassing the famed 'big five' of the animal kingdom (lion, elephant, buffalo, leopard and rhino), is second only to that of Kenya and can be seen and enjoyed on safari excursions that evoke the romantic world of Haggard and Hemingway. Here you'll find the classical veld, raw, sunblistered, sometimes savage in its primeval rhythms, often beautiful, always fascinating. To explore it on foot or by rugged four-wheel-drive, to wait quietly at a water hole as the four-legged parade arrives for its evening drink, to see the sun set explosively over river and limpid lake, and then to gather around the sociable campfire with a glass of good cheer in your hand, the stars above and the sounds of the African night all around – this is to experience the *real* Africa, and to garner images that remain as memory long after you have departed this enchanted land.

Zimbabwe has other and, in their own way, equally compelling faces, notable among which are the scenically superb Eastern Highlands region, the broad and inviting reaches of Lake Kariba, the ancient and mysterious stones of Great Zimbabwe, the great granite fastness of the Matobo Hills, and the modern, clean-lined cities of Harare and Bulawayo.

Zimbabwe is a young nation – it gained its freedom only in 1980 – but an old country. It was once the domain of the San (or Bushmen), small bands of hunter-gatherers who were supremely skilled in bushcraft and who roamed the great sunlit spaces in their ceaseless search for sustenance, living in harmony among themselves and with the world around them. These early inhabitants, the 'beautiful people', had a profound respect for their environment: to them, nature was sacrosanct, its integrity hallowed in the mystical rites of the hunt and the protracted, trance-like dance, and in the animated paintings that still decorate many cliff faces and cave walls.

Later on came other peoples, taller and darker Bantu-speakers who herded cattle, cultivated the land, knew the uses of iron and, because they were better organized and more aggressively territorial, eventually replaced the San as the dominant human presence. The first of the newcomers began to arrive from the north about 2 500 years ago, to be followed by the ancestral Shona who, over the centuries, evolved a highly civilized society centred around Great Zimbabwe, the huge stone citadel near today's Masvingo in the country's south-central region.

These settlers, the Shona-Karanga, drew their prosperity from the fertile cattle-sustaining grasslands of the area, from its generous deposits of gold and from their increasingly lucrative contacts with the Arab, Indian and Chinese traders of the East African coast. Between the 11th and 15th centuries the Rozvi – the dominant section of the Shona-Karanga – sustained a flourishing, militarily powerful empire that stretched from today's Botswana east to the Indian Ocean and from the Zambezi River south to the Limpopo. But then, sometime in the 1400s, the empire, due largely to economic factors, began to splinter into different groups and slide into decline. In the north the breakaway Mutapa dynasty grew strong while in the west, the natural heirs of Great Zimbabwe, the Torwa, built in stone at Kame and flourished. Later came the Rozvi predations and finally the emergence of Nguni invaders from the south.

The last and most warlike of the latter were the Ndebele, an offshoot of the eastern Nguni of South Africa's Natal region, whose leader Mzilikazi had quarrelled with the Zulu overlord Shaka and fled northwards with his 'raiding kingdom'. In due course the Ndebele's quest for a new home led them into conflict with and defeat by the Voortrekkers of the Transvaal, and in 1837 Mzilikazi crossed the Limpopo River and into the region to the south of modern Bulawayo. There, close to the great convulsion of hills known as the Matobos, he laid the foundations of a formidable militaristic state whose power and prestige remained virtually unchallenged for the next half-century and more.

In 1890 Cecil John Rhodes, the man who made millions from the Kimberley diamond fields and whose obsessive empire-building vision encompassed, among other things, a trans-Africa highway running from the Cape to Cairo, sent his 'Pioneer Column' of white settlers north into Mashonaland. By the end of the decade the colonists, soon to be known as Rhodesians, had crushed armed uprisings among both the Shona and the Ndebele and were in control of the whole of the territory that is now Zimbabwe. The colonial era lasted for 90 years, during which time the fledgeling country – after initial setbacks, not the least of which was their inability to source the gold they had come to find – began to develop, its modest prosperity based on mining (initially of gold, later of coal, chrome, asbestos and iron ore), on ranching and on the fruits of the fertile land. Most lucrative of the latter have been the splendid harvests of tobacco, exported in quantity (Zimbabwe is the world's largest exporter) since the early decades of the century.

For most of that period Southern Rhodesia (the name was formally conferred in 1911) remained a peaceful little corner of Britain's empire, a backwater which was largely ignored by its titular masters in far-off London. Real authority lay with the colonial politicians and their settler constituency. The black people – always an overwhelming majority (whites never numbered more than a quarter of a million) – had very little say in government, were deprived of most of their land and largely excluded from the economic mainstream. In 1922 the white electorate rejected union with South Africa and, during the following year, Southern Rhodesia became a self-governing colony. Three decades later, however, it did take part in a merger, joining its two northern neighbours to form the Federation of the Rhodesias and Nyasaland – an uncomfortable arrangement that provoked bitter opposition from an African nationalist movement that was just beginning to flex its muscles, and which was determined on independence.

When the federation was finally dismantled in 1963, Northern Rhodesia and Nyasaland gained full autonomy as Zambia and Malawi respectively. Racist Southern Rhodesia was denied similar status – the British government insisted on guaranteed moves towards democracy as a precondition – and in November 1965 premier Ian Smith and his right-wing Rhodesian Front party declared the colony's sovereign independence. This was a unilateral decision, condemned by the world at large, and Rhodesia remained in a state of siege for 15 years. For a while the rebels managed (with South African help) to withstand both international sanctions and guerilla infiltration but eventually the pressures told and, in 1979, national economic exhaustion and declining white morale forced Smith to the negotiating table. The following year, after the ground-breaking Lancaster House conference in London, the country was readmitted to the community of nations as the Republic of Zimbabwe – a fully democratic state whose first leader was Robert Mugabe. Such, in the briefest terms, is the historical background.

The ruins of Great Zimbabwe (above) stand as mute and grand testament to the power, the prosperity and the skill of the ancient Shona-Karanga. The city, which is thought to have had a population of some 40 000, was once the fast-beating heart of an empire that stretched from today's Botswana east to the Indian Ocean, and from the Limpopo River north to the Zambezi.

An elderly Shona man poses with his hunting spear (below). Seven out of ten Zimbabweans live in the rural areas, but, as in most parts of the developing world, there is a relentless drift of people to the cities.

The evangelical religious movement is strong in Zimbabwe (bottom); biblical-style robes, open-air worship and charismatic leadership are common to the various groups.

*M*odern Zimbabwe has a population that will soon reach 13 million, about 70 per cent of whom belong to the various Shona groups (five main ones in all) of the central and eastern areas. Half of the remainder (16 per cent of the total) are of Ndebele stock, based around the southwestern city of Bulawayo, and there are small minorities of Venda, Sotho, Tonga and Hengwe. Like many parts of the developing world, 'urban drift', the large-scale movement of people from the countryside to the cities, is a feature of the Zimbabwean scene – Harare receives 60 000 immigrants from rural areas each year – and the ancient cultures are being eroded, the fabric weakened by intensive exposure to the blessings and curses of the acquisitive society.

There has, however, been a startling revival of Shona sculpture, and the age-old skills of pottery, weaving and basketry, each drawing on the bounty of the veld for its materials, still flourish in some of the remoter areas. Much else is being preserved artificially and in isolated form – most notably at the Victoria Falls, whose multi-cultured craft village functions as a splendid showplace of tribal lifestyles, customs, architecture, ornamentation, dance and drama. The intangibles of indigenous culture – religious faith, social values and status, the communal ownership of land, the complex bonds of kinship and so forth – have proved a lot more durable.

Around 75 per cent of the population belongs to one or other of the Christian churches, but Christian teaching coexists with and, in many instances, is woven into the body of traditional conviction. Central to the latter is the concept of an all-knowing and ever-present (though somewhat remote) Creator, known to the Shona as *Mwari* and to the Ndebele as the *Mulimu*. Other prominent elements of religious practise include the veneration of ancestors, who have a powerful influence on the health and general well-being of their lineage and through whom prayers to *Mwari* are channelled, and spirit mediums or diviners (the *n'angas*, incorrectly termed 'witchdoctors' by some outsiders), who act as intermediaries between the dead and their living descendants. Many mediums are also healers, who treat the sick with herbs and other medicinal flora collected from the veld.

Lastly, and in common with most religions in sub-Saharan Africa, there is animism: the belief that natural features and phenomena – trees and rivers, hills, rocks, the wind and so on – have personas, or souls. The majority of Zimbabweans (about 70 per cent) still live in the country, their lives deeply rooted in the soil, and it is to the rural areas that one must go to understand these dignified, gentle, good-humoured people. In many village communities personal wealth continues to be measured in livestock, which often forms the currency that cements family relationships. When a young woman is betrothed, for instance, her family will get together with the groom's kinsmen to negotiate the bride price, or *lobola*, and the dowry is still, in many places, calculated and paid over in cattle.

For day-to-day sustenance, though, the villagers are dependent not on meat but on the maize (or 'mealies') grown on their communal lands. Agricultural reform is among the government's most urgent priorities, and since the early 1980s, thousands of country folk have moved into the cash economy by growing maize commercially and by turning over their fields to tobacco, barley, cotton, groundnuts, sunflowers (whose seeds are rich in vegetable oil) and other 'difficult' crops. But these pathfinders remain in the minority, and subsistence farming is still the norm across most of the country.

The domestic scene is simple. The country homestead has changed little over the decades: sleeping huts are invariably round (they're known to townsmen as 'rondavels'), their walls made of smooth mud or, more usually nowadays, of home-made bricks, capped with a cylinder of thatch, their floors of baked earth, their doors facing west to keep out the prevailing, though rarely uncomfortable, easterly breezes. There's usually a separate kitchen area, often a small granary, sometimes a cattle kraal. Village routines are leisurely, predictable, governed largely by the seasons.

*I*n the long, dry months of winter, lumbering herds of elephant migrate northwards from the Kalahari sandveld of northern Botswana into the Hwange National Park, Zimbabwe's premier wildlife sanctuary and one of Africa's finest game reserves. They are drawn to the area by its water pans (man-made and pump-supplied reservoirs, though they look natural enough) and by its sparse but sweet grasses, and at times the park plays host to 20 000 and more of these animals, which is rather more than Hwange can comfortably accommodate.

Elephants are gentle creatures, but highly destructive in their habits. To sustain its immense bulk, a full-grown adult consumes up to 250 kilograms (551 pounds) of grass, leaves and stripped bark each day, and will bring down an entire tree in order to get to the few tender shoots at the top. If the herds are allowed to become too large, the effect on the environment can be devastating, posing a threat both to the elephants and to the survival of other species. Their numbers, therefore, have to be controlled, and this means periodic culling, all of which has its controversial side, but what it does signify is that Zimbabwe's conservationists are – in one respect at least – holding their own. This is in marked contrast to the situation in much of the rest of Africa to the north, whose total elephant population has fallen from 1.3 million to around 600 000 in less than two decades.

Hwange occupies an impressive 15 000-square kilometres (5 792 square miles) of sun-baked terrain in the far northwest corner of Zimbabwe, a woodland region interspersed with broad grassland plains, bush and scattered stands of hardwoods such as teak and false mopane, that nurtures as great a density and variety of wildlife as any other conservation area in Africa. This abundance is due, in part, to its geographical location: it is the meeting point of two groups of fauna, the place where the animals of the Kalahari drylands mingle with species suited to moister, better endowed habitats. Among the park's larger residents are giraffe (around 3 000 of them), buffalo, zebra, wildebeest and 16 of southern Africa's 33 types of antelope, including the stately, curve-horned sable, the roan, the hartebeest and tsessebe, the graceful little impala and the gemsbok, a hardy, drought-adapted species that has made its home in the Hwange's southwestern corner. And, of course, wherever the plains game go you'll find their attendant predators – lion, leopard and the occasional cheetah, swiftest of all land mammals, wild dog, spotted hyaena and its elusive brown cousin. All in all, 25 different kinds of carnivore hunt and scavenge in Hwange's great spaces.

The rhino's story makes unhappier reading than that of the elephant. The most endangered of Africa's larger mammals, rhinos were introduced into the park during this century: the environment is ideal for them and, all things being equal, they would have flourished. But the demand for their horns – used in the Far East in medicinal preparations and in some Arab countries for ornamentation – remains unchecked and poachers have all but wiped them out, not only in the Hwange but elsewhere. Indeed, the only black (or hook-lipped) rhino now to be found in the wild – other than those on private estates – are those few kept under intense, armed and radio-tagged observation in one area of Hwange and three other parks in Zimbabwe – a total of 300 black altogether.

Most of the park – the flattish grassland, scrub and forests that cover the central and southern parts and which drain into Botswana's Makgadikgadi basin – remains a pristine wilderness where the animals roam at will, undisturbed by any significant human presence. Tourism is largely confined to the far northern segment, a distinctive and fairly well-watered region (it's part of the Zambezi watershed) of rugged outcrops and mopane woodlands. Here there are three largish and four smaller, exclusive public rest-camps, all linked together by nearly 500 kilometres (300 miles) of dirt roads that lead to picnic spots and view-sites, most of which overlook water holes.

Game-viewing is something of an art. Generally speaking, water holes are a lot more rewarding than the exploratory drive: it's a waiting game and one has to be patient, of course, but there's always something to be seen at the water's edge – a mongoose perhaps; a ground hornbill; a briskly busy family of warthogs with their long, thin tails held characteristically erect; a bateleur riding the thermals high above. And sooner or later the larger animals will appear on parade – zebra, antelope, a group of elephant seeking the coolness of mud and water, a pride of regally disdainful lion, perhaps a lone leopard, a bevy of gentle giraffe. These last, beautifully dapple-patterned and tallest of all the animals (bulls reach a height of around 5.5 metres; 18 feet), are especially fascinating to watch as they bend down, with legs splayed wide, to drink. The best times to visit a water hole are in the early morning and late afternoon: the game (and sensible game-viewers, too) tend to lie up during the heat of the day.

The camps are pleasantly restful places, comfortable, shady, well-founded. Accommodation is in self-catering cottages, chalets and lodges. Main, Robins and Sinamatella camps have restaurants, licensed bars, shops and fuel, although Robins Camp is rather less sophisticated; all three, together with the much smaller venues – Bumbusi, Lukosi, Nantwich and Deka – offer splendid game-viewing in their immediate vicinities. At Main Camp you can observe the animals by moonlight from a viewing platform above one of the water holes – an unforgettable experience.

More exclusive are the half-dozen or so private lodges that lie along and close to the park's boundary in the southern Dete Vlei section near Main Camp, places that provide comfort, fine food and wine, attentive service and the ultimate in game-viewing luxury (professional guides, who know exactly where to locate the animals, take you out in custom-built safari vehicles). Sable Valley Lodge's beautifully thatched, pink-slate-and-hardwood buildings, well sited among the shade trees

Cape buffalo are silhouetted against the darkening sky in the Hwange National Park (above). Only the northern section of this splendid sanctuary has been extensively developed for tourism; the much larger southern region remains a pristine wilderness in which the animals remain virtually undisturbed. Much of the wildlife – notably the elephant herds – migrate with the seasons, moving off into northern Botswana with the coming of the rains.

to afford maximum privacy, hosted Queen Elizabeth II and the Duke of Edinburgh on their visit to Zimbabwe in 1990. Hwange Safari Lodge – which is in fact a biggish three-star hotel with all the conventional amenities – is notable for its magnificent viewing platform, part of the bar area, that overlooks the floodlit water hole. At Sikumi, Kanondo and Ivory Lodge you sleep in teak-and-thatch tree houses, each with its *en suite* facilities that, at Sikumi, even include electric blankets in winter. Jabulisa Camp (the name means 'place of happiness') is a converted 1920s farmhouse surrounded by a scatter of cabins charmingly furnished and decorated in an attractive African style. Each venue has its own, distinctive character; all offer the holiday of a lifetime.

*A*n original way of visiting Hwange is to join the five-day steam train safari that begins and ends in the city of Bulawayo, 250 kilometres (155 miles) to the southeast. It stops at the village of Dete on the park's boundary for afternoon and evening game-viewing and then goes on to the Victoria Falls early the next morning. Passengers spend the nights either on board, in the most elegant of vintage settings, or at one of the private lodges. The steam locomotives are among the largest ever built, the food cordon bleu, the champagne breakfasts memorable.

The Falls area also has wildlife interest. Flanking the river upstream is the 57 000-hectare (140 847-acres) Zambezi National Park, haven for four of the 'big five' (the exception is, as always, the rhino) and umpteen others, many of which you can see on the 46-kilometre-drive (29 miles) along the river's luxuriant frontage. En route there are 20 or so shady riverbank spots where you can stop for a picnic, or to fish in the broad, slow-moving waters. An alternative 25-kilometre-game drive (16 miles) cuts through the park's southern section.

The majority of visitors, though, are drawn to the area by its other attractions, most notable of which are the Falls themselves. They're at their most spectacular just after the end of the rainy season (that is, between February and May) when the six great cascades roar tumultuously over the 1 700-metre (5 577 feet) rim to form the world's largest continuous curtain of water (each minute's volume would be enough to satisfy the needs of a city like Johannesburg for an entire year). From September through to November, the period of lowest flow, most of the water finds its way over the Devil's Cataract, leaving several of the other falls virtually dry. Even at this time, though, the bare faces have their special grandeur.

Newcomers invariably catch their first glimpse of this majestic scene from the rain forest (a World Heritage Site), a lush enchantment of fairytale glades nurtured by the rising mists of the cataracts and the ceaseless 'rain' of fine droplets they create. This magical little world – it covers just over 2 000 hectares (4 942 acres) fringing the Falls and extending over a narrow strip along the Zambezi's southern bank – has been set aside, as the Victoria Falls National Park, to protect both the aspect and the forest's plant and animal life. Small though it is, the park embraces a marvellous profusion of living forms. Here, made luxuriant by the moisture and the rich humus underfoot, are dense banks of ferns counterpointed by the brightness of wild orchid, aloe and flame lily. Impenetrable tangles of creeper and vine mantle giant strangler figs and ebonies, mahoganies, palms and sausage trees. The butterflies are a joy. A myriad birds – fire finches and blue waxbills, the rare turaco, the lovely paradise flycatcher and Heuglin's robin among them – bring flashes of animated colour to the deep-green dimness.

A path through the forest takes you to the very edge of the gorge; steps lead down the cliff-face to an observation platform overlooking Devil's Cataract. There are a number of other splendid viewpoints, among them the Victoria Falls bridge that connects Zimbabwe with neighbouring Zambia. The railway link – part of Cecil Rhodes's grand but never realized Cape-to-Cairo route – was finally completed in 1905 and, for that time, represented a remarkable feat of engineering. It would have made a lot more sense to have built the bridge upstream but Rhodes, normally the epitome of ruthless practicality, was overwhelmed by the beauty of the Falls and insisted on the more scenic approach. He died three years before the first train puffed its way over the gorge.

Curiously enough the Falls, greatest of Africa's natural wonders, remained refreshingly untouched by commercialism for nearly six decades, despite their fame, their obvious tourist potential and ever-improving communications. A small township did develop

The magical sunset hour at Chizarira Wilderness Lodge (below), a secluded private camp within the Chizarira National Park near the upper reaches of Lake Kariba. The countryside here is rugged, untamed, home to elephant, buffalo and a multitude of antelope. Lodge guests are conducted on game drives and walking safaris.

close to the crossing, but up till the 1950s this comprised little more than a few curio outlets, a trading store and that grand old lady of the hospitality business, the Edwardian-colonial Victoria Falls Hotel. The scene today is very different. Victoria Falls, with a permanent population of around 10 000 and a transient one of several thousand more, is well served by amenities – shops, a supermarket, restaurants, banks, service stations and a bustling international airport. The original hotel, since modernized but as gracefully attractive as ever, has been joined by half a dozen sophisticated and, some of them, supremely luxurious establishments that offer all the comforts and conveniences. Visitors spend their days viewing the splendour of the tumbling waters, relaxing at the poolside, playing golf (wildlife is a novel feature of the fairways), and exploring the river reaches in various ways – the energetic on foot (some lovely walks have been charted), the adventurous by canoe or raft, the self-indulgent on the marvellously sociable sunset cruises or, even more hedonistic, the wine canoe route. There are also excursions by air: the 20-minute 'Flight of Angels' light-aircraft flip offers a brief but unforgettable bird's-eye-view of the awesome cataracts.

Evenings are taken up in wining, dining, gambling, being entertained, with perhaps time out to watch the eerie lunar rainbow that often appears in the misty moonlight above the great chasm. Not to be missed are the barbecues and displays of traditional dancing held on the sweeping lawns of the oldest hotel. There's African dancing, too – among much else – at the 'living museum' cultural village (*see* page 54). Well worth a visit is the local crocodile ranch, whose pens hold up to 10 000 of these primeval creatures.

*T*ravel 150 kilometres (93 miles) downstream from the Falls and you'll reach the western extremity of what until recently was the largest man-made lake in the world, a 280-kilometre-long (174 miles), 40-kilometre-wide (25 miles), beautiful stretch of water that is both a wildlife paradise and one of Africa's premier leisure areas. Lake Kariba was created in the later 1950s – a time when the short-lived Federation of the Rhodesias and Nyasaland still held some promise for the future – both as a bountiful source of hydroelectric energy and a symbol of regional unity. It was an impressive project, grand in conception, brilliant in execution – and enormously costly, not only in terms of money but in human life as well. It transformed the face of the land and its demographic character: more than 50 000 Gwembe Tonga tribesmen had to be moved away from their ancestral fishing and farming grounds ahead of the rising waters, and local sages warned of the displeasure of *Nyaminyami*, the river god, and of the vengeance he would exact on the meddlesome intruders. It may have been coincidence that unprecedented floods damaged and almost destroyed the half-built dam, killing 17 of its workers. Altogether, more than 70 people died during the four-year construction period.

The expanding lake also threatened the teeming wildlife populations of the area. Many of the animals managed to retreat to safety but others were trapped on the shrinking patches of dry land. Most of these – some 5 000 in all – were rescued by Rupert Fothergill and his rangers during Operation Noah, a marvellously quixotic and internationally publicized relocation exercise that still enjoys an eminent place in conservation lore.

In May 1960 Queen Elizabeth, the Queen Mother, formally inaugurated the dam, a massive, 128-metre-high (420 feet) concrete arch spanning the 600-metre (1 969 feet) gorge that divides Zimbabwe from Zambia. By that time the lake was already extensive, its islands well-defined, the dying trees along its widening shores beginning to assume their skeletal shapes. Today Kariba is virtually an inland sea: its 160 billion cubic metres of water have inundated 5 180 square kilometres (2 000 square miles) of wild African countryside, and to skirt its perimeter on foot would – if you were eccentric enough to make the attempt – involve a 4 000-kilometre-trek (2 485 miles). Most visitors explore the area by boat, confining themselves largely to the better developed eastern end. One of the quicker and more comfortable ways of gaining a proper perspective, of seeing the lake as a whole and enjoying some of its many splendours, is to board the regular car ferry at Kariba's busiest harbour, Andora, near the dam wall, for the 22-hour voyage to Mlibizi in the west.

On the Heights above the wall is Kariba town, a pleasant little centre originally established to house the largely Italian artisan workforce that built the dam. They also built the Church of Santa Barbara, a charmingly unusual structure of mostly open archways in place of walls, though some of the arches are enclosed with stained glass (each of these colourful panels bears one line each, in Latin, of the Lord's Prayer). Also worth a sightseeing hour is the nearby crocodile farm, where these giant prehistoric reptiles are bred for commercial and restocking purposes. Here you can buy well-crafted handbags and other attractive leatherwork at fairly reasonable prices.

Inviting alternatives to land-based living at Kariba are provided by the various cabin-craft available for hire. They include the fairly standard cruise-boat (above) with its elevated deck, shady aftdeck and two or three cabins. Some of the larger models incorporate a surprisingly spacious saloon with television and hi-fi. Quite different are the small, pontoon-type houseboats designed for those who wants the best of both water and wilderness, comprising little more than roughly built wooden cabins and a viewing deck.

A distinctively patterned moth (above) displays its colours against one of the Hwange park's hardwoods.

A collection of Tonga weapons and implements (opposite). The Tonga of the Zambezi Valley in the northeast are fisherfolk and hunters by tradition but when the rising waters of Kariba forced them off their ancestral lands, many adapted to an agricultural lifestyle.

But it is the lake itself that draws the attention, and the holidaymaker. The broad, breeze-blown, sometimes storm-tossed but usually placid waters and their wild surrounds are a mecca for yachtsmen, canoeists and aquatic sports enthusiasts, for game-viewers, bird-watchers and for thousands who simply like spending long, lazy days soaking up the sun. And for fishermen: the lake sustains 40 or so different kinds of fish, among them the deep-bodied and delicious tilapia (also known as Kariba bream) and the fighting tigerfish so favoured by serious game anglers. More valuable in practical terms are the tiny, sardine-like *kapenta* that the lakeside villagers, most notably the residents of Msampa, net in huge quantities: the harvest, which averages about 12 000 tonnes a year, is sun-dried and sold in the wider market to supply much-needed protein to Zimbabwe's poorer communities.

Scattered among the bays and secluded inlets of the southern shore are pretty little harbours and marinas bright with leisure craft; hotels that offer comfortable and in some cases – at Bumi Hills, Fothergill Island, Gache Gache and the Caribbea Bay resort and casino, for instance – luxurious living; and safari lodges embraced by the magic of the wilderness. And then there are the houseboats, mostly small and unpretentious craft incorporating a twin-bedded cabin, dressing room, kitchen nook, shower, chemical toilet and game-viewing deck. You'll often find three or four of these boats moored inshore, huddled close to their 'mother ship' to form a floating safari camp. In the evening guests paddle or row across to the larger vessel to linger over sociable sundowners and dine under the stars.

Other boats are more sophisticated, varying in design from the smallish and cosy to impressive 12-berth affairs of spacious *en suite* cabins and saloons complete with television and hi-fi sets. Invariably there's an upper deck equipped with shade canopy and sun-beds, and an after-deck that serves as dining room and cocktail bar. Life aboard is supremely relaxed, the routine flexible and undemanding: spending mornings fishing, canoeing, exploring the shoreline, game- and bird-spotting, communing with the quieter spirits, getting together for companionable lunches, sleeping them off in the heat of the afternoon, partying at night. Included in the holiday package are various 'specials' – a trip up to the Victoria Falls, for example, or into one of the region's splendid game parks; a bush trail; a white-water rafting excursion down the Zambezi, and so forth. Two companies offer sailing safaris using either catamaran or monohull craft, probably the very best way to explore the vast waters, the silence and shoreline game of Kariba.

Biggest of the boats, and in a class of its own, is the 50-metre-long (164 feet), multi-decked *Southern Belle*, a Mississippi-type paddle steamer (the paddles are for show only) that boasts 20 cabins and four elegant staterooms, a spacious restaurant, splash pool, games deck and delightfully evocative Victorian decor.

The lakeside is a treasure-house of wildlife. Crocodiles bask and hippo wallow in the shallows; the rich mix of aquatic and land grasses, particularly the emerald green torpedo grass (*Panicum repens*) that flourishes between the high- and low-water marks, attract elephants, buffalos, giraffes and a host of other animals. Much of this wonderfully wild kingdom is conserved within a number of extensive reserves and safari areas, most prominent of which is the rugged, 1 370-square kilometre (529-square mile) Matusadona National Park.

The magnificent Matusadona wilderness fringes on the lake's eastern basin, sprawling southwards over the dense woodlands and bush-covered slopes of the dramatic Zambezi escarpment. The Ume River forms part of the park's western boundary; the eastern is delineated by the Sanyati and its precipitous gorge; in between are great, unspoilt spaces that serve as sanctuary for a splendid array of game animals. The human presence tends to be concentrated around the estuaries, bays and attractively vegetated offshore islands of the northern part (this is where Tashinga, the park's main public camp, is located) where there are luxury lodges and attractive camping sites, but one can explore the interior by four-wheel-drive or on one of the organized wilderness foot trails.

Even wilder is the Chizarira National Park, a remote expanse of msasa-mantled hillside and plunging valley to the southeast of Kariba's upper reaches. From the heights there are fine views across to the distant lake and down to the rugged terrain of the Chete, one of the Zambezi region's several safari areas (these are conservancies which have not been developed for general tourism, though sporting hunters are allowed in under strictly controlled conditions). Another such area, the rather more accessible Charara, extends from the eastern end of the lake – the dam wall and Kariba township are at its northwestern corner – to provide a popular venue for shore-anglers and the more adventurous of game viewers. Its one camp, Nyanyana, lies at the river-mouth and is sometimes visited by elephants. A special treat, not far from Kariba town, is the Wildlife's Society's spectacular Kuburi Wilderness Area.

uch of the land downstream from Kariba – a region known as the middle Zambezi valley – has been set aside for the wildlife and the preservation of its habitats. Here you'll find the superb Mana Pools National Park and five pristine safari areas which, together, cover almost 11 000-square kilometres (4 247 square miles) of riverine and rugged escarpment countryside. The region is one of Africa's last great wildernesses; its six conservancies are collectively recognized as a World Heritage Site. For man, the low-lying Zambezi valley has its dangers and discomforts, prominent among which are the tsetse fly (which causes sleeping sickness), the malarial mosquito, the bilharzia snail and other tropical infestations. For much of the year the air is suffocating in its superheated humidity; the terrain difficult, the internal routes sometimes – in the rainy season – impassable. But, for all that, the river reaches and their flanking hills have their beauty and their interest, and are an irresistible attraction for both the serious environmentalist and the ordinary visitor who wants to experience raw Africa at its most magnificent.

After leaving Lake Kariba the Zambezi tumbles through a narrow gorge and then widens to run north across a broad, flattish flood plain. Over the millennia its course has meandered, the sluggish waters leaving behind great quantities of rich alluvial soil and a myriad shallow channels and seasonal pools. These fertile riverine terraces, which extend for several kilometres southwards, sustain a lush ground-cover of grasses and forests of acacia, mopane and huge mahogany trees.

This luxuriance is a magnet for the animals of the region. During the dry months the herds come down from the hills in search of water and good grazing, and to be there in the weeks before the onset of the summer rains (usually in November) is to witness an unforgettable spectacle. The middle Zambezi is home to more than 12 000 elephants – the world's largest concentration outside the Hwange National Park – and most of them seem to be gathered on the terraces. Other large mammals are there in almost equal profusion: 2 000-strong herds of buffalo that darken the sun with the dust of their passage; zebra, kudu, eland, impala and an array of other antelope; ubiquitous baboons, monkeys, warthogs. And always, hovering close by, sleekly confident of their prey, are the predators – lion and leopard, hyena and wild dog and the symbol of Mana, the ferocious little honey badger. Goliath herons, storks, cormorants, spurwing and Egyptian geese flap and fossick at the water's edge; vultures swoop and settle; the imperious fish eagle watches intently from its riverside perch before planing down to the surface and, without pause in its flight, grasping the meal of the day in its powerful talons.

A wondrous wilderness indeed. But, like so many other of Africa's treasure-houses, one under constant threat. Poachers cross the river to make savage inroads into the herds; the rhinos of the area have disappeared; tsetse control measures will, if carried out as planned, pave the way for domestic cattle – perhaps the quickest and certainly the surest path to environmental destruction. Moreover, there have been proposals to dam the river upstream at Batoka Gorge, so drowning the terraces. And it's just possible that commercially viable oil deposits may be found deep beneath the surface. For the time being, though, the integrity of Mana Pools and its neighbours remains intact: a wild country both of great beauty and of profound significance in the natural scheme.

Mana Pools is served by two unpretentious but attractive public lodges and, farther down the river, a caravan and camping ground. The best times of the day for game-viewing are the very early morning and mid- to late-afternoon, when many of the animals emerge from their hillside cover and onto the terraces. Most visitors explore the park via its rather challenging road network; some prefer to find their way around on foot: this is the only Zimbabwean big-game area in which you're allowed to walk unaccompanied (but do so with the utmost caution, bearing in mind that practically any creature can be dangerous if startled, or separated from its young, or cut off from its line of retreat). You can also take to the water by boat or canoe, which offers a splendid alternative to the game drive and bush trail. The fishing along the park's forest-fringed river frontage is excellent and a must for any keen angler.

And here too, as in nearly all the country's game areas, there's an inviting choice of private safari lodges. Chikwenya, at the confluence of the Zambezi and Sapi rivers in a splendidly unspoilt area of riverine forest and game-filled flood plain, has Tonga-style semi-open chalets which enjoy unrestricted views of the waters. Ruckomechi Camp, set in truly magnificent big-tree country, looks across the river to the high Zambian mountains. In 1995 it won Zimbabwe's title of best safari camp for the third year running. Its thatched bar, dining and relaxation complex – the latter a sociable deck arrangement where guests meet together at the magical sunset hour – also looks over the river. These venues employ resident guides who take you on drives and walks, on boating and canoeing trips. For fishermen and bird-watchers, the expeditions into the watery wilderness are occasions to be savoured and remembered.

The handsomely embowered Busi bush-camp (above), on the Busi River within the Chizarira National Park. The area, close to the upper reaches of Lake Kariba, remains refreshingly free of commercial development.

A strikingly original carving (below), on view in Harare's Chapungu Sculpture Park. The Shona school of contemporary sculpture is, according to *Newsweek* magazine, probably the most important art form to have emerged from Africa during the 20th century.

The endangered and beautiful cheetah (above), swiftest of all land mammals. The species is easily recognized by its lithe, spotted body, long legs, small head, rounded ears and by the two 'tear marks' running from the eyes to the mouth. The 'king cheetah', occasionally found in Zimbabwe, is a rare genetic variant whose spots merge together in attractive bars and streaks.

Zimbabwe's capital and by far its largest urban centre is Harare, located almost 1 500 metres (4 921 feet) above sea level on the mostly clear-skied Highveld ridge in the country's northeastern quadrant. The wider metropolitan area (including Chitungwiza dormitory town to the south, the country's third largest city) covers a lot of ground and accommodates nearly a million and a half people, but the central business district is small by international standards, neat, bustling with traffic, comprising just a score or so symmetrically arranged blocks of handsome buildings. Among the more eye-catching of the edifices are the new cylindrical Reserve Bank building, the highest in the country, the skyscraping, scoop-shaped and luxurious Monomotapa Hotel and, along Samora Machel Avenue to the west, the ultra-modern, internally gold-panelled International Conference Centre – which is geared to host 4 000 delegates at any one time – and the next-door Sheraton Hotel.

Many of the city's thoroughfares, and the avenues that cut through the extensive residential flatlands to the north and east, are graced by splendid flowering trees – feathery, lilac-blossomed jacarandas and blood-red flamboyants for the most part. The former come into bloom in the springtime (September to November), the flamboyants a little later to cover city and suburb in riotous colour. Other species are, if not quite so prominent, common enough and as lovely in their season: bauhinia and mimosa, poinsettia and great billows of bougainvillea everywhere you look.

Around 750 tree species are indigenous to Zimbabwe, and a great many of them can be seen in the National Botanic Gardens, 4 kilometres (2.5 miles) to the north of city centre. Most common of the Highveld's trees are the msasa and its look-alike, the mnondo, both of which grow to a stately 6-7 metres (20-23 feet) and, come August, enchant the eye with the exquisite russets and golds of their foliage. There's floral interest of a quite different kind 40 kilometres (25 miles) distant at the Ewanrigg Botanical Gardens, a pleasant 250-hectare expanse (618 acres) of natural vegetation embracing a cultivated area renowned for its aloes and a variety of other endemic plants. Rather special are the cycads, those 'living fossils' that were flourishing a full 150 million years ago and which reached their ascendancy before the first flowering plants appeared on earth.

Other destinations popular among nature lovers include the scenically appealing Mazowe area, an hour's drive to the north of Harare. Here there are orchards of scented citrus, avocados and mangoes, granadillas and litchis and other tropical fruits, lush fields of cotton and maize and hill upon rolling green hill. Also worth an excursion is Lake Chivero to the west, originally created as a national park but now one of the region's most popular recreational areas. The placid waters entice anglers, yachtsmen and watersport enthusiasts; the adjacent, densely wooded game reserve is haven to white rhino and buffalo, giraffe, leopard, baboon, wildebeest, eland, kudu reedbuck and other antelope. For visitors, there's a pleasant rest-camp and, along the lakeshore, a hotel, caravan parks, picnic spots, swimming pools, a tea garden and a marina.

But back to Harare itself. You'll also find natural beauty in the lawned and embowered municipal gardens, an oasis of tranquility in the heart of the city and the setting for the attractively designed National Gallery. The building is the home of modern Zimbabwean stone sculpture, a strikingly original art form that began to develop in earnest during the 1960s and now commands international acclaim. Zimbabweans feature in, even dominate, the upper echelons of the world's leading sculptor-carvers, their dark, brooding, atavistic works on public display in galleries from Tokyo to New York. A number of other local venues feature the Shona school of art, among them the rather less rarified Chapungu village centre, a five-hectare (12 acre) sculpture garden, located in Harare's Msasa suburb, that also encompasses a typical Shona rural settlement, and which features traditional dancing at weekends.

There's sculpture, too – though of another kind and created for another purpose – within Heroes' Acre, which was established in the 1980s as a national shrine, cemetery and memorial to those who worked, fought and died for Zimbabwe's liberation during the *chimurenga* war. The complex and its impressive monument to the unknown soldier, high on a hill just outside town, is a grand affair of terraces, a long staircase, soaring obelisk and various impressive pieces of statuary and monumental stonework, some of which draws part of its inspiration from the Korean co-designers of the monument rather than from Africa. A museum is planned, but the Acre remains private, even hallowed ground. Permission is necessary but easily obtained from the Ministry of Information in town.

Another prominent hill, the boulder-strewn and green-mantled Kopje on the city's southwestern fringes, also has its place in the annals, though its relevance relates to a time fast receding from the collective memory. It was beneath this granite outcrop, on the 'beautiful open plain with rich red soil', that Cecil Rhodes's colonial adventurers ended their 600-kilometre odyssey (373 miles) on 12 September 1890. They named their camp Fort Salisbury in honour of Britain's prime minister of the time, and on the following day hoisted the Union Jack in what is now Africa Unity Square (formerly Cecil Square). The Kopje, one of the few natural landmarks in an otherwise flattish cityscape, has long served as a popular vantage point from which to survey Harare and the surrounding countryside, but may soon have prouder status: it has been earmarked as the site of Zimbabwe's new (but as yet uncommissioned) parliament building.

*S*tand atop Mount Inyangani and the whole of Africa, it seems, unfolds before you. To the east, the land plunges precipitously to the heat-hazed plains of Mozambique, a country until recently riven by civil war but peaceful enough now and beautiful, to the distant spectator, in its mantle of greenery. To the west the heights tumble to rounded foothills and deep woodland valleys, beyond which is the broad patchwork spread of the highveld farmlands. Northwards, the eye takes you across the plateau to the misty magic of the Troutbeck downs; southwards, far below, lies the sunlit, tropically luxuriant and marvellously fertile Honde Valley.

Inyangani, at 2 592 metres (8 508 feet) above sea level, is Zimbabwe's highest mountain and the most striking single feature of the great upland rampart that runs for 300 kilometres (186 miles) along the country's eastern border. It dominates the Nyanga region, northernmost of three related but distinct sections of the great mountain wall. Much of this lovely land is embraced by the Nyanga National Park, whose open grassland slopes, pine plantations and occasional patches of montane forest, its entrancing waterfalls, tranquil dams and cold, clear, trout-filled streams, have passionate devotees among both the hiking and angling fraternities. Most impressive of the falls are those of the Pungwe (the largest of the region's 17 rivers), which thunders over the high lip of the escarpment in a massive cataract to enter the 10-kilometre-long (6 miles), densely wooded gorge. Not quite as dramatic but equally eye-catching in its own way is the nearby Mutarazi Falls, a long, thin, silver ribbon of water that drops down more than 762 metres (2 500 feet) – which makes it Zimbabwe's highest and Africa's second highest – to the rain forest in a setting of pure enchantment.

The Nyanga area, like its neighbours to the south, is charmingly developed for tourism, its best-known hostelry the old-established and elegantly country-style Troutbeck Inn. The hotel offers a golf course, a trout-stocked lake and unpretentious luxury in the most splendid of surrounds: in the hills above are the placid waters of the Connemara Lakes and the well-named World's View, which commands the most breathtaking of vistas across the highveld plateau. Here, too, there's a tumble of ruins, one of literally hundreds of ancient stone structures – sunken enclosures, stock pens, *kopje* forts, terraced retaining walls – that were built by the long-gone Iron Age farming communities. Many of the sites now do duty as picnic sites and observation points; the Ziwa Museum will give you a sharp insight into ancestral lifestyles. The Nyahokwe mountain ruins nearby, a must for those interested in archaeology, are a stiff climb, but one enhanced by the enthusiastic (and somewhat romantic) commentary of the guide who leads you up.

The summit of Inyangani peak (above), in the Nyanga National Park at the northern end of the eastern Highlands, is Zimbabwe's highest point: it rises 2 539 metres (8 508 feet) above sea level, dominating a land of high hills, deep and lovely valleys, misty heaths, plantations, natural forests, mountain streams and waterfalls. Largest and most spectacular of the cascades are the Pungwe, the Nyangombe and the Mutarazi.

Tea plantations are an economically important feature of the Eastern Highlands. Especially notable are the emerald harvests of the Honde Valley (below); other valuable crops include coffee and subtropical fruits. The upland region, embracing the Nyanga, Bvumba and Chimanimani mountains, is famed for its wild flowers, among which is the colourful Chimanimani sugarbush (above).

Mutare, Zimbabwe's fifth largest urban centre, capital of and gateway to the Eastern Highlands and known as Umtali in the colonial days, is a lovely little city almost entirely surrounded by high mountains. The town does full justice to its setting: streets are lined by tall palms and by jacarandas and flamboyants; suburban gardens are bright with the strident colours of bougainvillea and other flowering plants. A small corner of the wider area is occupied by the grounds of the La Rochelle estate, once owned by wealthy industrialist Sir Stephen Courtauld, bequeathed to the nation and, though perhaps a little run down now, is still graced by an exquisite profusion of orchids, rare trees and ornamental shrubs. It also features a braille wilderness trail, one of only two in southern Africa. To get to Mutare you have to negotiate Christmas Pass, the loftiest point on the main highway that leads from Harare eastwards to the Mozambican port of Beira.

Mutare is one of Zimbawe's more prosperous towns, its wealth derived from its strategic position astride the tourist and trade routes, and from the richness of a Manicaland countryside given over to forestry, cattle, tobacco, seed potatoes, cut-flower proteas, coffee, subtropical fruit and, above all, splendid plantations of emerald green tea bushes. It also has its industries, among them textiles, clothing, leather goods, food processing, vehicle assembly and oil refining. Zimbabwe's second university has been established just to the north.

The town guards the northern shoulder of the Bvumba range of mountains, gentler than their Nyanga neighbours, more lushly covered and in their own, Scotch-misty way just as beautiful. And well served by hotels, among them the White Horse Inn with its cosy, country-house atmosphere and stunning terrace views, the award-winning Inn on the Vumba, and the pink-turreted, castle-like Leopard Rock, whose broad acres encompass a fantasy of rocks, giant and twisty strangler figs, a wealth of water features and a challenging 18-hole golf course looking out to unparalleled mountain vistas. On the Royal visit to Zimbabwe (then Southern Rhodesia) in 1953, Queen Elizabeth, the present Queen Mother, described Leopard Rock as the most beautiful place in Africa.

For the leisurely motorist, the Bvumba offers a cornucopia of delights. First suggested port of call are the Bvumba Botanical Gardens, a smallish expanse of quite entrancing highland countryside that includes a 30-hectare (74 acres) area cultivated in English-country style, its pathways, streams and ponds girded around by fuchsias and azaleas, lilies and hydrangeas. Rather larger and of a quite different character is the nearby Bunga Forest Reserve, sanctuary for an array of indigenous trees, ferns, flowers, butterflies and birds. Drive down the Bvumba's western slopes and you'll find yourself in the 12-kilometre-long (7 miles) Burma Valley, a moist and astonishingly fertile lowland swathe whose generous bounty includes tea, tobacco and bananas and the much sought-after range of 'Vumba' cheeses. Above the valley, on the wooded hillsides sweeping up to a lofty ridge called Himalaya, are cedar and yellowwood trees, everlastings, proteas and arum lilies.

The third and southernmost component of the Eastern Highlands is a gigantic and lichen-covered granite wall, mantled by twisted mountain msasas rising into the mists, whose Zimbabwean section (two thirds of the range lies within neighbouring Mozambique) is largely embraced by the Chimanimani National Park. This is a wild and lovely land of high peaks (three of them exceed 2 200 metres; 7 218 feet), craggy outcrops and ravines, of a myriad perennial streams and their magical waterfalls. Notable among the latter is the Bridal Veil cascade, 5 kilometres (3 miles) from Chimanimani village and part of a fairly extensive sanctuary originally set aside for the conservation of eland – the only large-sized antelope that flourishes among pine plantations. The Bridal Veil cascades lie close to the headwater of the Nyahadi River and to get there involves a short but rather rough drive along a gravel road; the journey is well worth the effort, though. You follow a footpath through pleasant picnic clearings and groves of acacia trees, two of which – one light-coloured, the other dark – twist together to create, in the eyes of an imaginative observer, a touching symbol of unity that has real relevance in Zimbabwe. At the end of the path there's a clear, limpid, fern-fringed pool and smooth boulders on which to rest and commune with the gentler muses. A magical place indeed. The wider area's floral character – proteas, ericas and everlastings are everywhere – is curiously reminiscent of the distinctive Western Cape countryside nearly 3 000 kilometres (1 864 miles) south.

A meandering, often mist-wreathed and scenically stunning road connects the village of Chimanimani with Chipinge, a busy little farming centre that thrives on the area's coffee and cattle farms and on its tea, pine and wattle estates. Beyond lies the Chirinda Forest Botanical Reserve with its magnificent trees, among them stately figs, ironwoods and mahoganies. The Big Tree, tucked away in the Valley of the Giants, is a 66-metre-tall (216 feet) red mahogany more than 1 000 years old. Delighting the eye, too, is a kaleidoscope of ferns and mosses, parasite creepers, orchids, pink Manica daisies, crimson flame lilies – and a myriad butterflies.

The southern third of Zimbabwe, from the Botswana border in the west across to Mozambique, is low-lying country, the southeastern segment known as the Lowveld – a sere, unforgiving region of leached soils, granite outcrops and gnarled old baobabs, of sparse grasses that sustain gaunt cattle, and of village communities that have learnt to live with drought, and with crushing poverty. Here, water is the most precious of all commodities. But the dreary tapestry has its patches of brightness. The Lowveld is cut through by two major rivers, though all too often their flows amount to little more than a trickle. The Save, second largest of Zimbabwe's watercourses, rises on the plateau between Mutare and Harare to run southwards, along the flanks of the Chimanimani foothills, joining the Runde close to the Mozambiquan frontier. These rivers, and their tributaries, have been harnessed to create a remarkably lush and hugely productive expanse of greenery, a healing lotion for the eyes in an otherwise formidably harsh land.

Studies undertaken just after the Second World War indicated that nearly 3 000 square kilometres (1 158 square miles) of the eastern Lowveld could be irrigated. Research stations were established, a campaign launched to eradicate the tsetse fly, and in the later 1950s the waters of the Runde, and those of Lake Mutirikwi (*see* page 148), were tapped to nurture Hippo Valley, the first of the citrus plantations. In due course sugar cane – much of it grown on the new Triangle estates – supplanted oranges as the principal crop, and fields of winter wheat were planted to add to the region's bounty.

The principal Lowveld centre is Chiredzi, a green-garlanded, fast-growing little place located on the edge of Hippo Valley, that still has something of the pioneer outpost about it. The sugar estates are beautifully run; a network of neat roads provides easy access; the local mill, geared to process 10 000 and more tonnes of sugar a day, is an impressive affair. The surrounding area supports a number of huge, private game properties known locally as conservancies, merging former cattle ranches and wildlife enterprises such as the Save Conservancy (Africa's largest), Lone Star and Bubiana. Some combine these with activities such as crocodile and ostrich farming (the low-calorie meat of these big terrestial birds is an increasingly popular item on menus around the world).

Graceful impala antelope graze beneath the Chilojo Cliffs in the Gonarezhou National Park (above), potentially one of southern Africa's finest wildlife sanctuaries. The most prominent of the park's other animals are its elephants, which migrate seasonally across the neighbouring borders.

The bateleur (below), one of the more easily recognised of Zimbabwe's birds of prey, is distinguished by its large wingspan, short tail and the black, chestnut and brown of its plumage.

For wildlife enthusiasts, though, by far the Lowveld's most compelling attraction is the Gonarezhou National Park, a ruggedly remote swathe of heat-blasted baobab and mopane terrain that covers 5 000 square kilometres (1 930 square miles) of Zimbabwe's south-eastern corner. The name in the local Shona-Ndao dialect means 'place of elephants', and this is indeed elephant country: for much of the time around 6 000 of the great, slow-moving pachyderms make their home in Gonarezhou, moving freely over national borders – into Mozambique and South Africa's famed Kruger National Park – as the seasons dictate. Though gentle enough in other parts of southern Africa, these particular elephants tend to be highly strung, unusually wary of intruders, largely because guns – semi-automatic AK47s for the most part – became so commonplace in the region during Mozambique's decades-long civil war. Even the official pamphlet warns that the animals 'bear a grudge against man due to persecution and harassment over the years ...'.

Gonarezhou also supports many other large species – buffalo and giraffe, zebra, hippo and crocodile along the reaches of the Save and Runde rivers, the shy suni, the oribi and rock-loving klipspringer, the rare Lichtenstein's hartebeest among them. Rather special are the handsome, shaggy-coated nyala antelope, once seldom seen but now prolific in the riverine belt. Carnivores include lion and the elusive leopard.

The best of the viewing areas is probably the Chipinda Pools section of the Runde in the north; a visually striking feature of the river is its spectacular series of red-sandstone Chilojo Cliffs, cut through by gullies along which the game animals make their way to reach the water. At the confluence of the Runde and Save is an 8-kilometre-long (5 mile) stretch of marshland that, at times, attracts a marvellous parade of birds. The southern part of the park, the Mabalauta section, is perhaps a little more difficult to explore but here, too, the grasslands sustain a fine array of animals. Elephant, buffalo and lion occasionally move through Swimuwini, the main rest-camp, and nyala are wont to drink at its fishpond.

Gonarezhou could have been developed into one of Zimbabwe's most outstanding game conservation enterprises, but there have been setbacks. Voracious herds of elephant and periodical bush-burning (part of the tsetse fly control programme) have damaged the vegetation; the Runde and Save have lost much of their life-giving water to the irrigated farmlands and plantations; poachers continue to do their worst, and periodic droughts take their grim toll of both the ground cover and the animals it supports. Still, the park remains a superb wilderness that might one day, with luck and proper management, rank among Africa's great eco-tourism destinations. Recently, the largest translocation of elephant ever undertaken moved 200 surplus Gonarezhou elephant to a reserve in northern South Africa.

Near Masvingo, in the south-central part of the country, is Mutirikwi (below), third largest of Zimbabwe's lakes and a splendid recreation area and game park. The reservoir supplies life-giving water to the huge sugar and citrus estates of the Lowveld.

A few kilometres from Masvingo in the south-central region lies a massive collection of stone ruins that have bequeathed their name to the country. Great Zimbabwe, haunting legacy of the once all-powerful Shona-Karanga kings, comprises three main elements: the Great Enclosure, the Hilltop Complex, and the myriad other smaller walled structures that occupy the valley in between. The walls and passageways of the *dzimba dzembabwe* – the 'houses of stone' – were fashioned from millions of interlocking pieces of granite, and have survived more or less intact for close on a thousand years, a remarkable testament to the skill of builders who knew nothing of the binding properties of mortar. Many of the structures are decorated with chevron, herringbone, dog's-tooth and other intricate patterns.

The Great Enclosure, which measures 243 metres (797 feet) in circumference and whose 11-metre-high (36 feet) walls encompass a solid conical tower (reminiscent of a giant grain-basket, symbol of abundance), is the largest ancient edifice south of the Sahara. It was the bastion of the royal Rozvi household, functioning as the heart of a settlement thought to have numbered around 40 000 people. It represents the highest point of Shona architecture, and provided the model for some 150 other major, though much smaller, stone sites scattered throughout the country.

The Hill Complex is rather older. An elaborate blend of stonework and balancing boulders, it has two sections and three entrances, and it may well have functioned as the religious centre of the community, home to its powerful spirit mediums. These ruins have yielded a wealth of intriguing archaeological finds, among them eight soapstone carvings of the famed 'Zimbabwe bird' – stylized, 30-centimetre-high (12 inch) respresentations of the fish eagle, believed to have been sacred to the Hungwe group of the Karanga people. Looted long ago by collectors, they have since been returned and occupy a prime position in the new walk-through and air-conditioned site museum.

Other artefacts – beads, pieces of pottery and glass – speak of more exotic roots, and indeed the first white travellers to visit Great Zimbabwe, and the colonial Rhodesian settlers who came after, speculated wildly about possible Phoenician, Indian, Arab and even Chinese origins. Others, among them novelists and adventurers with a literary inclination, wrote of the Land of Ophir, King Solomon and much else in the realm of romantic fantasy. But in fact Great Zimbabwe is entirely African in conception, execution and character, its main structures erected between AD 1000 and 1200 to flourish until the late 1400s as the powerhouse of an indigenous empire that covered a huge expanse of south-central Africa. Your tour of the site will also take in the splendid aloes which grow in profusion in the valley between Great Zimbabwe and the Hill Complex.

A short drive to the northeast of Great Zimbabwe will bring you to the country's third largest reservoir. In years of good rains Lake Mutirikwi's waters extend across 90 square kilometres (35 square miles); its dam wall rises 63 metres (207 feet). It was built (in the 1960s) to feed the Lowveld's vast sugar and citrus plantations, though it is more familiar to the public as an attractive and pleasantly developed recreational area. The lake itself, known as Kyle in the pre-independence days, sustains hippo, crocodile and a wealth of aquatic creatures; its many islands are home to an impressive diversity of birds; among residents of the adjacent game park are white rhino, buffalo, giraffe, wildebeest, zebra and a wider variety of antelope than you'll find in any other Zimbabwean park. The wildlife suffered grievously during the crippling droughts of the 1980s and early 1990s – years during which the lake virtually dried out and the surrounding veld became a parched wasteland. In good times, however, the abundant waters welcome yachtsmen, powerboat enthusiasts and black-bass fishermen. On and near the shores are boat moorings, caravan and camping sites, hotels and a well-appointed rest camp.

Discerning anglers also beat a path to the Mushandike sanctuary 30 kilometres (19 miles) southwest of Masvingo. Centred on a tranquil, hill-flanked lake, this multi-purpose area combines wildlife conservation with research and education (it accommodates the country's National Resources College), game farming and recreation.

The 440-kilometre-long highway (273 miles) that leads southwest over the flattish, often cosmos-graced grasslands from Harare to Bulawayo passes through three of Zimbabwe's more substantial towns, unpretentious hubs of commercial and industrial activity that don't have too much to offer the leisure-bent traveller.

Kadoma, the first you get to (after about 100 kilometres; 62 miles), started life in 1906 as a railway siding, called and known for more than half a century as Gatooma, which grew up around the area's modestly profitable gold diggings. Other minerals – notably nickel, chrome and magnesite – have since been found and are being exploited, but the town now derives most of its income from its textile mill and the surrounding cotton fields.

Kwekwe, the second port of call and rich in both minerals and farmlands, lies almost exactly half way along the route and is rather more attractive, a pleasant place of flowering trees and lawn-fringed, shady streets. Its name, originally spelt Que Que, is taken from the local river (the word is immitative, representing the croaking of frogs that live in and around the waters), and it too owes its origins to the turn-of-the-century gold workings. A special feature of interest in town is the National Gold Mining Museum, whose unusual centrepiece is a prefabricated and imported (in 1894, from Britain) 'paper house' that served as home to the early plant managers.

Gweru (formerly Gwelo), the third and largest of the centres and venue of the country's military museum, has a solid industrial base that includes railway marshalling yards, mines – the region is rich in asbestos, tungsten and limestone – and a variety of manufacturing enterprises, among them a factory that produces 10 million pairs of shoes a year. Gweru also features modestly in the military annals. The clear, wind-free skies and the flattish terrain prompted the establishment of an air force training school during the Second World War. Later, the facilities provided the focus of the colonial (and rebel Rhodesian) air arms, and latterly of the Zimbabwean air force.

In a different class is Bulawayo, second largest of Zimbabwe's cities, capital of the Matabeleland Province and a moderately attractive, rather sprawling metropolis of modern buildings and some rather graceful colonial edifices; of broad, jacaranda-lined thoroughfares that were originally designed to allow 24-span ox-wagons to manoeuvre in comfort, and of some of the loveliest public gardens in the country. Bulawayo was founded in the early 1870s by the Ndebele king Lobengula, Mzilikazi's successor, and named in commemoration of his battlefield triumphs (the name means 'place of slaughter'). Two decades later, during the punitive Matabele war, Rhodes's invading settlers put the 20 000-strong, mud-and-thatch settlement to the torch, forcing the king into a lonely and soon enough fatal exile in the remoteness of the Kamativi region far to the northwest. The whites erected their own wattle-and-daub houses in its place and then, for some curious reason, moved the entire town to a new site – the present one – about 5 kilometres (3 miles) away.

Today Bulawayo is a city of some half-million people – most of whom belong to the Ndebele group – and the headquarters of the country's extensive rail system. The 2 745-kilometre-long network (1 706 miles) is largely diesel-operated, but some steam locomotives still do honourable private rail safari duty and can be seen at the local yards. Worth a special visit is the Railway Museum, which houses a splendid collection of the old work-horses together with rolling stock and machinery dating back to the very early years. Bulawayo's industrial spectrum also encompasses an impressive number and variety of secondary enterprises – textiles, building materials, vehicle assembly, radios and other electronic products, printing, packaging and food processing, banking and insurance.

One of the city's most enduring problems is a perennial shortage of water: this is a hot, dry region located on the fringes of the Kalahari, and drought has been the norm rather than the exception over the past decade or so. Indeed, only two seasons during a recent 15-year period brought adequate rains, and as the crisis deepens so the proposed remedies become more ambitious. The ultimate solution, according to local experts, is to siphon water from the Zambezi, which lies a formidable 400 kilometres (249 miles) to the northwest but, if harnessed, could ensure and enrich the future: just 90 seconds of the river's prodigious flow would satisfy Bulawayo's entire yearly needs and, moreover, irrigate the surrounding and usually parched farmlands.

For all its thirst, though, Bulawayo puts on a remarkably fresh and colourful face. Brightly blossomed trees grace the avenues, the suburban gardens are a joy, and a broad, green lung, which flanks the Amatsheumhlope River, bisects the city. One part of the latter is taken up by the tall shade trees and exquisite roses of Central Park; another by lovely Centenary Park's emerald lawns, its aviary, game enclosure, theatre and National History Museum. Pride of the museum is its 75 000-item collection of mammals, the largest in the southern hemisphere; among the more intriguing exhibits are a mounted

Giraffe (below) are an elegant feature of Zimbabwe's game areas. They're usually found in herds of up to 20 individuals, feeding on the tender leaves of trees and, occasionally, on new grass. Their main predator is the lion, and they are at their most vulnerable while drinking at river or water-hole – they have to bend down to the water, with their forelegs splayed wide, which more or less immobilizes them. Still, they're by no means easy prey, even for the big cats. Away from water they are masters of camouflage, fleet of foot, and able to deliver a lethal kick with both fore- and hindlegs.

elephant of 3 metres (9 feet), the 2 000-year-old egg of a giant and long-extinct Madagascan bird, and an array of artefacts from Great Zimbabwe and other ruins.

The ancient terraces of Kame, second in size only to Great Zimbabwe and a proclaimed World Heritage Site, sprawl over a hillside 16 kilometres (10 miles) from Bulawayo. The stone-walled structures were among the last and most impressive built by the Torwa group of the Shona-Karanga culture: they made their appearance during the 15th and 16th centuries, and the community flourished until first the invading Rozvi and later Mzilikazi's Ndebele occupied the land in the late 1830s. For decades afterwards Kame was held as the 'king's preserve' – hallowed ground, venue for sacred ceremonies and hidden from prying European eyes until Rhodes's mounted columns rode in during the 1890s. Visitors get to the Hill Ruins – the most striking of Kame's five complexes – via a rocky pathway flanked by euphorbias, monkeythorns, purple-pod acacias and marula trees. There's also a site museum whose displays include ancient pottery decorated with graphite (black) and haemotite (red), carved animals and soapstone pipe-bowls. Among other artefacts unearthed by the archaeologists are glass beads, some surprising fragments of Ming porcelain and, oddly, a spoon originating in 17th-century Europe.

To the African people, Kame is still a place of profound mystical significance. So, too, are the Matobos to the south of Bulawayo, a region

The countryside around Harare is distinguished by eye-catching 'balancing' rock' formations. This one (above) is among many within the 40-hectare (25 acre) Epworth Mission area 13 kilometres (8 miles) south of the city. The haphazardly arranged granite slabs are the product of millennia of erosion during which the elements – wind, rain, heat and cold – crumbled away the surrounding ground.

of massive and immensely ancient granite domes, whalebacks and craggy heights, and of caves and cliff faces decorated by those most marvellous of prehistoric artists, the San. The Shona-Karanga venerated the place, their oracles receiving the words of *Mwari* among the huge and hauntingly beautiful tumble of hills. Later came the Ndebele, whose leader gave them their current name: it translates as 'bald heads' because the rounded formations reminded the great soldier-king of an assembly of his elderly counsellors. Mzilikazi chose to be buried here, and it was to this fastness that Lobengula's warriors retired to make their last stand against the invading white forces. Here too, at a series of dignified *indabas* in 1897, Cecil Rhodes finally made peace with the Ndebele.

Rhodes, too, is buried in the Matobos – in a simple grave, set within a natural amphitheatre of boulders, at the top of a height named World's View. All around, and to the horizons, colossal landscapes of granite hills rise and spread. Much of the area – 43 000 hectares (106 253 acres) in all – falls within the Matobo National Park, a grand haven for the zebra and giraffe of the grasslands, for the leopard that stalks the rockier parts, and for the black eagle that rides the high thermals.

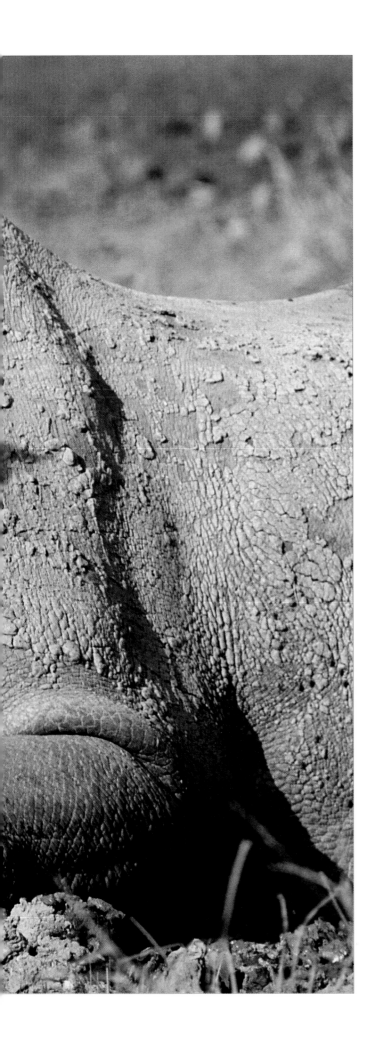

KINGDOM OF THE WILD

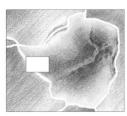

A little more than a century ago Zimbabwe's finest sanctuary served as the royal hunting preserve of the great Ndebele warrior-king Mzilikazi and his successor Lobengula, who took their pick of the game on their sporadic expeditions into the western wilderness and then departed, leaving this vast land of sand and scrub to the teeming herds. But then came the white men with their cattle, their rifles, their greed for ivory and their passion for 'sport', and the animals – most of them – disappeared. It was only in the 1920s, after the reclusively eccentric rancher Herbert Robins had converted his property into a wildlife haven, that the authorities began to appreciate the region's potential. They took over one of Robin's ranches (he relinquished it in exchange for a new house and water system) and in 1928 formally proclaimed a reserve. Hwange, then known as Wankie, became a national park in 1949.

When Hwange's first warden, Ted Davison, surveyed his domain in the late 1920s, he found it virtually devoid of the larger game species. The animal populations had suffered grievously from indiscriminate hunting and, in the 1890s, from a particularly savage outbreak of rinderpest, but the real enemy was drought: the Kalahari sandveld could not sustain surface water, its ancient rivers no longer flowed and the seasonal pans filled only after the rare and brief rains. So Davison devised a system of boreholes to feed both the natural pans and the 60 or so new ones he created, and the game reappeared.

Today, at peak occupancy – the numbers fluctuate according to migration patterns – the park supports upwards of 17 000 elephants, 15 000 Cape buffalos, 3 000 giraffes, rhinos from time to time (their story has not been a happy one), wildebeest, the stately sable and the rare roan antelope, kudu, tsessebe, impala and many other herbivores, together with their attendant predators, most prominent of which are the lions and leopards. Indeed, Hwange boasts one of the largest concentrations of game animals anywhere in Africa.

Hwange's white rhinos (left) – which, together with their black cousins, were reintroduced into the park – are ideally suited to the environment but, as in many other parts of Africa, poachers have taken a devastating toll of their numbers.

Ivory Lodge (opposite), part of a chain of luxurious private safari venues located along the northern perimeter of Hwange, provides an atmospheric setting for the classic African bush experience; guests sleep in rustic but comfortable tree houses.

Larger and more conventional is the park's Main Camp (below), one of three major and four smaller public rest-camps within the park and close to its northern boundary. They are linked by some 500 kilometres (300 miles) of well-maintained gravel roads.

Road-signs on the main highway (right) connecting Bulawayo, Hwange and Victoria Falls warn of the presence of the Cape hunting or wild dog (far right), one of Africa's most endangered species. Pack-hunting wild dogs have a remarkably intricate and finely balanced social organization.

Part of Hwange's vast population of elephant (opposite) gathers at the Caterpillar Pan. They share the golden evening with a herd of wildebeest, seen in the background.

Hides and observation points are strategically sited along game-viewing routes; one of the most rewarding is that at the Mataka water hole (above).

Tallest of Hwange's residents are the giraffe (right): bulls grow to a height of between 5 and 5.5 metres (16 and 18 feet). Here, a quartet slakes its thirst at one of the many artificial (but natural-looking) pans.

The beautiful cheetah (above) is the fastest of all land mammals – it can reach speeds of up to 100 kmph (62 mph) in short bursts – but is also one of the most vulnerable. The animal hunts its prey, usually impala, springbok and other medium-sized antelope, in dramatic, high-speed chases across open grassland country.

A far more familiar sight in Hwange park is the Burchell's zebra (right), which congregates on the flattish savanna plains. These close relatives of the horse are often joined by wildebeest and antelope, perhaps because their keen hearing and eyesight provide early warning of, and therefore protection against, predators on the prowl.

Hwange is home to more than 400 different kinds of bird, including bateleurs and other splendid raptors. Among the smaller species is the lilacbreasted roller (opposite), a member of a colourful family of little perching birds that earn their common name from their display flights: they roll and tumble like miniature aerial acrobats.

Water lilies (above) bring a splash of colour to the pan near Sinamatella. Hwange has no perennial streams: the wildlife is sustained by the standing water in the natural pans, and in the pump-supplied dams.

The view from Sinametella's terrace (right). Sinametella, sited on a boulder-strewn plateau overlooking a valley rich in game, is one of Hwange's larger public rest-camps, each of which comprises self-catering cottages, chalets and lodges, a restaurant, bar and shop. The camps, though, have their own, distinctive characters and attractions: Main is the starting point of nine separate game-viewing drives; Robins is famed for the lions that tend to congregate in the immediate area; Sinamatella for its leopards and its game routes, most notably that known as the Lukozi Loop.

Robins Camp (below), the least sophisticated of Hwange's three major venues (the original farm-house forms part of the complex) is tucked away among the mopane trees of the northern region. Hwange's forests, in fact, are rather special, graced by Zimbabwe teak (known locally as *mgusi*), giant red mahoganies and their Natal cousins, African ebonies and wonderbooms. A number of the trees bear edible fruits; notable is that of the marula (whose nuts are also rich in protein).

Big Tom's water hole (opposite), named after one of the two ranches that were converted into the original game reserve, plays host to impala and sable antelope. The sable, with its long, scimitar-shaped horns and large (1.3-metre-tall; 4.5 feet) body, is an especially striking looking animal, living in herds numbering 10 to 30 individuals. The smaller impala, a common enough sight in parks throughout southern Africa, is notable for its acrobatic grace when in flight.

Chacma baboons (left) are ubiquitous residents of Hwange, though they're most often found in the hillier, rockier parts. They are daytime feeders, omnivorous, their varied diet embracing wild fruits, bulbs, roots, scorpions, insects and even such vertebrate animals as birds, scrub hares and, occasionally, young antelope.

The baboon's chief enemy is the leopard. This infant (above) belongs to a small litter – up to three young are born at a time – whose cubs will grow into powerful and skilled nocturnal hunters. Leopards are agile climbers and will use the fork of a tree as a 'larder' in which to store the uneaten remains of a large kill.

One of Hwange's armed and well-trained game wardens (right), guardians of Zimbabwe's priceless natural heritage and the first line of defence against poachers.

Over the years Hwange's elephants (above and far right) have flourished – a triumph for conservation that stands in marked contrast to the situation in much of Africa to the north of the Zambezi. Indeed, over the past few decades the continent's total elephant population has declined by more than half. More than 17 000 of these gentle giants are in residence during the dry season, though when the rains come many of them migrate across the border into Botswana, drawn by the life-giving waters of the Chobe and Linyanti rivers.

A nonchalant yellow-billed egret (right) stands its ground a metre or so clear of an elephant's huge forelegs.

Most powerful of Hwange's 25 different kinds of carnivore, and largest of Africa's predators, is the lion (opposite), found throughout the park. Visitors are more likely to see these big cats in the Robins Camp area than elsewhere, and may – if they're lucky – chance upon a hunt and kill. The hunt is a complex process, one in which the female invariably plays a leading role: the male tends to be somewhat indolent. But his strength, when he is called upon to use it, is phenomenal. He is also able to show an astonishing turn of speed, covering 100 metres (330 feet) in just four to six seconds.

The whitefronted bee-eater (left) is a familiar resident of the Hwange park. These colourful little birds are most often seen along the steeper sandbanks of rivers and pans.

Female kudu (below) on the broad grasslands of Hwange. The male of the species is larger (he weighs in at about 225 kilograms; 496 pounds) and has horns.

THE SMOKE THAT THUNDERS

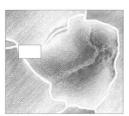

Few destinations in Africa, indeed in the world, can offer the traveller so much interest and visual delight as the Victoria Falls and their immediate surrounds. The area's focus, the grand central spectacle, is of course the series of immense cataracts that plunge thunderously over the 1 700-metre-wide (5 577 feet) cliff edge and down into the deep gorges at the rate of 500 000 cubic metres (17.6 million cubic feet) a minute during the peak flow period. The spreading spray – the Falls are known to the local Kololo people as *mosi-oa-tunya*, 'the smoke that thunders' – nurtures a rain forest of exquisite beauty, an enchanted place of ferns and giant sycamore figs, ebony, mahogany and palm trees. Meandering paths lead you through the dense undergrowth to the finest of views.

The Falls can best be seen in their grand totality, perhaps, on one or other of the aerial excursions on offer, among them the short 'Flight of Angels' fixed-wing and helicopter trips. Two microlights also do sightseeing duty, and commercial companies run wider-ranging air safaris that take in the Falls area. More leisurely are the various river rides, which range from a brief three-kilometre (two mile) jaunt to a three-day expedition that starts far upstream, at the Kasangula forests. Much favoured are the popular and sociable sundowner cruises which take you over the broad waters above the Falls as the last of the golden day casts its magical light over the river, its islands and forested fringes.

Fine hotels, glittering gaming rooms, show bars, superb golfing, river-rafting – visitor amenities and diversions at the Falls are varied and enticing. But you'll also find, here and there, a touch of the *real* Africa – on your drive through the game-rich Zambezi National Park stretching along the river to the west; in the many-cultured Craft Village, and in the vibrant displays put on by spectacularly talented traditional dance troupes.

The Makishi dancers (left) evoke the spirit of ancient cultures at the Falls Craft Village and Victoria Falls Hotel, with bizarre costume, music, comedy and vibrant dance.

Sightseeing by microlight (above) contains echoes of David Livingstone's 'flight of angels' who, he mused, must have gazed upon the Falls in all their loveliness. Livingstone first saw the cataracts in November 1855 but he did not 'discover' them. Khoisan, Kololo, Losvi, Tonga and Ndebele people had known them long before, and it is likely that Arab traders, Portuguese pathfinders and even Boer wanderers had preceded the great missionary-explorer. But it was Livingstone who first introduced them to the reading public of Europe and North America.

The 1 700-metre-long (5 577 feet) 'lip' of the massive Zambezi gorge at Victoria Falls (opposite) has, over the ages, been eroded into a number of segments, clefts and islands, directing the river's flow into separate cataracts – Devil's, Main, Horseshoe, Rainbow, Armchair and Eastern. The immense surge of water is caught up in the deep, narrow chasm between the Falls and the opposite, parallel cliff wall, along the top of which is the entrancing rain forest (part of the Victoria Falls National Park). April is the month of peak flow.

The sunset view (left), from above the Victoria Falls, of the gorges, Livingstone Island and the famed railway bridge. The latter, a magnificent feat of engineering for its time, was a vital link in the Cape to Cairo route that tycoon and controversial empire-builder Cecil Rhodes dreamed of. He lived long enough to have the final say on the bridge's exact location – below the Falls, to afford travellers the most spectacular of views – but died three years before its completion in 1905.

'No-one can imagine the beauty of the view from anything witnessed in England' wrote David Livingstone, whose bronze likeness surveys the Falls (above). Livingstone embarked on a number of exploratory expeditions through central and East Africa, his most notable the four-year odyssey that took him first to the Atlantic settlement of Luanda and then inland along the Zambezi River, past the Victoria Falls, to the river's mouth on the Indian Ocean.

A shy bushbuck (above) browses in the dark-green depths of the rain forest that flanks the Falls. Trees, ferns, vines, wild orchids and thick undergrowth are nurtured by the myriad and continuously falling droplets of spray thrown out by the cataracts. A path leads through the area, a proclaimed national park, to the edge of the gorge.

Among the rain forest's many avian residents is the black-and-buff coloured Heuglin's robin (left). Falls and forest are recognized as a World Heritage Site.

Canoeing (opposite) and white-water rafting (overleaf) are among the more adventurous ways of exploring the mighty Zambezi – both above and, perhaps more challenging, below the Victoria Falls. The sport, though, is less dangerous that it looks. The river, Africa's fourth largest watercourse, rises in the uplands of Zambia, flowing south and then east to form the border between Zambia and Zimbabwe. It then enters Mozambique to discharge into the Indian Ocean, 3 540 kilometres (2 200 miles) from its source.

The Crocodile Ranch at the Zambezi Nature Sanctuary is home to more than 10 000 of these primeval reptiles, ranging in size from five-metre (16 feet) giants to small 50-centimetre-long (20 inch) hatchlings (left).

The ancient art of basket weaving (below) as demonstrated at one of the prime attractions of the Victoria Falls area, the Craft Village. This multi-faceted exposition of traditional skills, arts and lifestyles brings the various rural cultures into sharp relief. Visitors are also introduced to an Ndebele *n'anga* or spirit medium (opposite) in his creeper-covered hut. He is surrounded by the mysterious tools of his calling, and if asked, will throw and read the bones for you.

The village is very much a 'living' museum, a vibrantly evocative display not only of architecture but of costume, ornamentation, music, mime, drama and, above all, tribal dancing. Prominent features include the 30 or so rural dwellings on view, simple homesteads that are nevertheless remarkably varied in design.

Much of the handwork on sale at Victoria Falls, and indeed at pretty well every tourist venue in Zimbabwe, can be classed as 'airport art', but the subjects are invariably beautifully crafted and hold real charm. Here a cheerful vendor poses with his herd of graceful giraffes (left). Favoured materials are the local and excellent hardwoods (teak, ebony) and soapstone. The latter allows for greater variety, and a fine individualistic piece can occasionally be found among the displays of standard carvings.

Most visitors to Victoria Falls spend their days taking in the splendours of the cataracts, game-viewing, golfing, wining, dining, playing the tables and generally relaxing in this sun-drenched and most beautiful part of Africa. A few, though, come for adventure and excitement, some taking to the waters on canoe or raft, others to the heights: bungi-jumping (below) from the bridge that spans the Zambezi (and links Zimbabwe with Zambia) is now a lively feature of the local scene.

Large and extremely luxurious is the Elephant Hills Hotel, which was destroyed by fire during the bush war of the 1970s and later rebuilt in distinctive style – the decor is Mediterranean with strikingly ethnic African undertones. Its attractive water complex (right) is the country's largest; its atrium encloses a miniature rain forest; its magnificent golf course was designed by Gary Player.

The Victoria Falls Hotel (far right), grand old lady of the Falls area, first opened its doors in 1905, the year the inaugural steam train puffed its way over the newly completed river bridge, and has been receiving the travelling public in style ever since. The place has been upgraded from time to time – it has a four-star rating and all the modern comforts and conveniences – but its essential, charming character remains intact: high ceilings, shade-dappled verandahs and other Edwardian features speak of a more leisurely, more graceful era. Cordon bleu cuisine is served in the elegantly appointed Livingstone Room and on the terrace; evening events include a sumptuous barbecue and a memorable display of African traditional dancing on the sweeping lawns. The hotel's long-serving doorman, Oddwell (right), is resplendent in a uniform embellished with colourful tokens presented by parting guests.

A riverboat (above) takes visitors for a sunset cruise on the Zambezi above the Falls. Here the broad waters are invariably placid: the river does not gather speed as it approaches the gorge – the first indications of the cataracts are a thunderous roar and the cloud of spray, often rising fully 300 metres (1 000 feet) into the air. River excursions are both fascinating and sociable: passengers enjoy sundowners as the craft glides past wooded banks and islands rich in wildlife. Hippos (left and right) are a familiar sight.

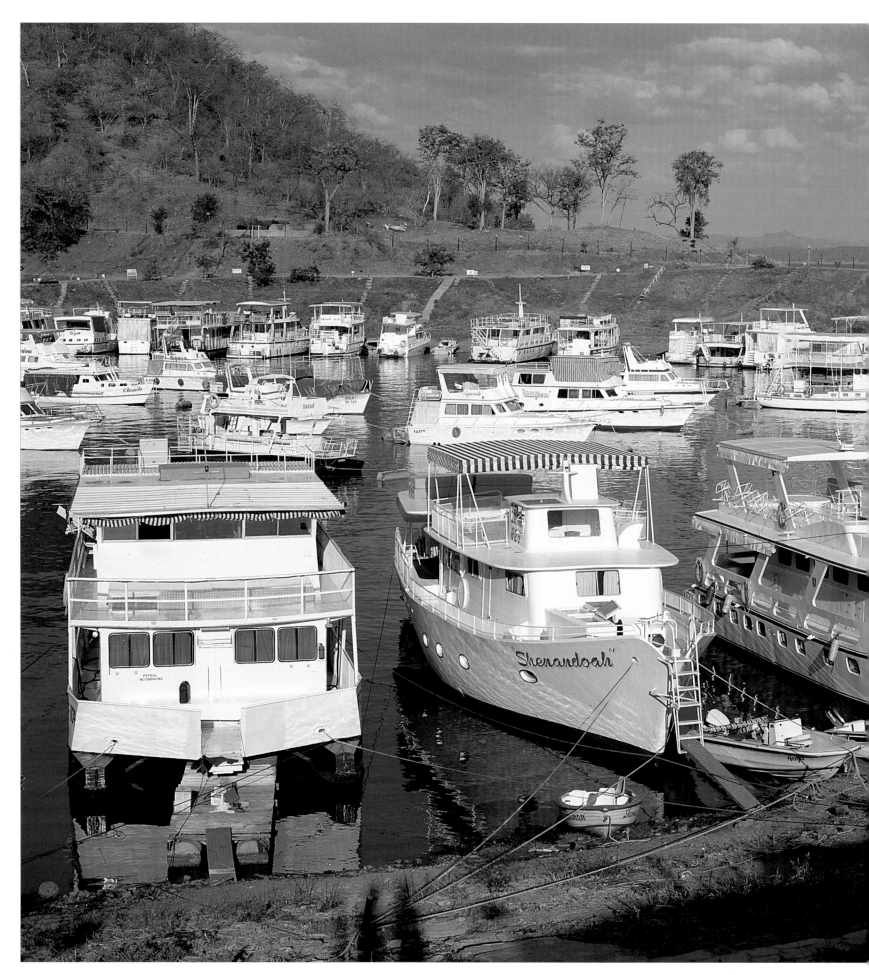

OF WATER AND WILDLIFE

Some 600 kilometres (373 miles) downstream from Victoria Falls the Zambezi River enters a narrow, cliff-sided gorge across which, nearly 40 years ago, a high, curving, concrete wall was built. The structure is 128 metres (420 feet) high, and its 633-metre-length (2 077 feet) is a conduit for a modern highway linking Zimbabwe with neighbouring Zambia. The wall created a great lake that stretches 285 kilometres (177 miles) to the west – an inland sea that now serves as one of Africa's foremost inland recreation areas.

Lake Kariba is a paradise for the more relaxed kind of holidaymaker, the one who likes messing about in boats, spending long, lazy hours in the sun, observing the myriad living forms of wild Africa. It's also a magnet for the keen angler: the waters, enriched by nutrients released by the drowned forests of yesteryear, are home to the fighting tigerfish and around 40 other freshwater species.

Along the lake's shoreline are creeks and inlets, marinas, resort hotels and lodges; two of the larger islands, Fothergill and Spurwing, support attractive safari camps. Many of Kariba's visitors, though, prefer to live on the water: there are dozens of houseboats and cruise vessels of different shapes and sizes available for charter, ranging from simple pontoon-type huts-on-floats to 12-passenger luxury craft complete with captain and crew. Among the biggest and most sophisticated of the boats is the paddle-steamer *Southern Belle*, a floating hotel that boasts 20 comfortable cabins plus staterooms (suites), a dining saloon, cocktail bar, pool and games deck.

Along and beyond the fringes of the lake sprawl some of Zimbabwe's finest game sanctuaries, among them the Matusadona National Park, haven for elephant, buffalo, zebra, hippo, giraffe, crocodile and a multitude of antelope. The lake's eastern extremity is flanked by the rugged Charara Safari Area; embracing the high hills of the Zambezi escarpment overlooking the lake's upper reaches is the equally splendid wilderness terrain of the Chizarira National Park.

Smart cruise-craft at their moorings in Caribbea Bay (left), close to Kariba town. Nearby is the sophisticated and popular Caribbea Bay hotel and casino resort.

Kariba's imposing dam wall (opposite), a 21-metre-thick (69 feet) concrete arch that towers nearly 130 metres (426 feet) above the narrow gorge through which the Zambezi once thundered, stands atop a massive chamber, carved out of solid rock, that houses the turbines and alternators of the hydroelectric power station. The complex was built, with the help of Italian engineering workers, during the 1950s and was plagued by unusually severe floods. Some 50 000 Tonga villagers were displaced by the spreading waters of the lake.

The inundations also covered an area teeming with wildlife, closing off ancient migratory routes and trapping a myriad animals on the shrinking islands. Much of the game – about 5 000 head in all – was brought to safety during the superbly organized rescue exercise known as Operation Noah. Development at the eastern end – notably the township of Kariba and its harbour – also upset the movement patterns of the herds, threatening access to water and prompting the authorities to declare much of Kariba a 'game corridor' (right).

Some of the inmates of Kariba's crocodile ranch (below). These giant reptiles (*Crocodylus niloticus*) are found in rivers and lakes throughout the subcontinent north of Zululand. The Nile crocodile, which can reach 6 metres (or more than 20 feet) in length, is a predator which is at its most active at night, spending most of the daylight hours basking quietly in the life-giving sun. Its varied diet is make up of fish, waterfowl, small animals and, occasionally, medium-sized mammals that come to the water's edge to drink.

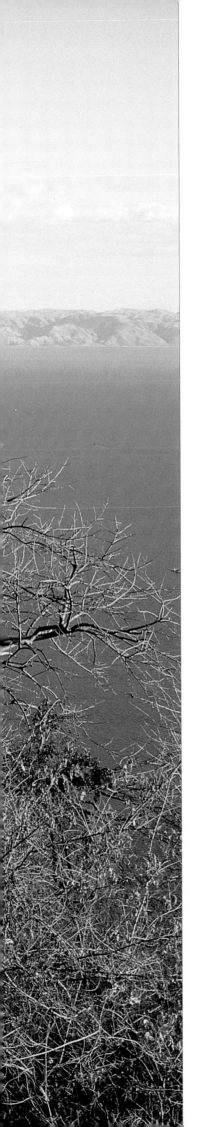

Magnificent views of the lake and its islands unfold from Kariba Heights (far left), an attractive residential area that boasts some smart houses, a hotel, a supermarket and an unusual church built to a circular, 'open' design that features archways instead of walls. Some of the carvings on sale at this and other popular viewpoints (below) have real artistic merit.

A familiar lakeshore resident and among the best-known of Africa's birds of prey is the fish eagle (left), a large and regal-looking raptor whose wingspan measures an impressive 230 centimetres (90 inches) and more. The eagle, as its name suggests, feeds mainly on fish, swooping down at a narrow angle to the water's surface and, without a pause in its flight, grasping its victim in powerful talons.

A safari boat from Fothergill Island Safari Lodge (above) introduces guests to two of the Matusadona park's elephants. The 400-hectare island (988 acres), named after the hero of the Operation Noah wildlife rescue mission, is large enough to accommodate its own big-game population plus some 25 Tonga-style lodges, a double-story central complex and a swimming pool.

Cape buffalo dot Matusadona's lakeshore (opposite), where the vegetation is a nutritious mix of aquatic and terrestial grasses. Hippos and crocodiles are commonly seen along the shoreline here; among the park's predators are leopards, hyaenas and lions (overleaf). Matusadona is the 'real' Africa, rugged, untamed and huge – it extends across 1 370 square

kilometres (529 square miles) from the fringes of the lake and up over the Zambezi escarpment. Visitors can explore the great spaces along wilderness trails and via one of two rudimentary roads. The latter, though, are usually closed off during the rainy season. Matusadona has three exclusive (block-bookings only) rest-camps, each of which can accommodate 12 guests.

Elephants amble in line along the water's edge (opposite) below Bumi Hills Safari Lodge in the western part of the Matusadona park. Bumu Hills is one of Kariba's most luxurious venues: more a hotel than a lodge, its beautifully appointed rooms are set high on a ridge overlooking the lake; guest amenities include game-viewing and sundowner cruises, exploratory walks, canoeing and fishing expeditions, observation hides and tree houses and, for those with time to spare, a four-day wilderness 'water safari' on specially designed lake craft.

A herd of watchful impala (above). When started into flight, these attractive antelope are sheer poetry in motion, making off over the veld, in perfect unison, in an almost ballet-like series of leaps and bounds.

Among the largest and most powerful – and, when threatened, dangerous – of Matusadona's residents is the Cape buffalo (right). Adult males weigh about 800 kilograms (1 764 pounds).

The skeletal remains of the long-dead forests stand like ghostly sentinels above the mirror-like surface of Kariba (right). Until recently, the lake, which covers more than 4 000 square kilometres (1 544 square miles) of the Zambezi Valley, ranked as the world's largest man-made expanse of water.

The catch of the day (above). The tigerfish, with its razor-sharp teeth and unquenchable spirit, is among the most sought-after game species on southern Africa's lakes and rivers. A number of fishing camps operate at Kariba and along the Zambezi, enticing the keener angler; the international tigerfishing tournament, held at Kariba each year, is rated the world's biggest freshwater angling contest by the Guiness Book of Records. About 300 teams compete for prizes.

The densely wooded hills of the Zambezi escarpment (opposite) to the southeast of Lake Kariba's upper reaches. Much of the area, a spectacular compound of msasa-covered mountain slopes and deep ravines, is occupied by the Chizarira National Park, a remote sanctuary difficult to get to and get around (a four-wheel-drive vehicle is almost mandatory) but well worth exploring. The park's wildlife complement includes some 1 000 elephants, about the same number of buffalo, roan, tsessebe, the handsome sable (right) and other antelope, lion and leopard and a splendid array of birds. Of special note are the crowned eagle, the bat hawk and the elusive Taita falcon. Overnight visitors have the choice of six exclusive camping sites, three of which offer sleeping shelters. More comfortable by far is the privately run Chizarira Wilderness Lodge, a smallish, attractive complex of stone-and-thatch cottages set among stately mountain acacia trees. The lodge's swimming pool, built among and blending into the rocky outcrops, is a notable feature.

DOWNSTREAM TO EDEN

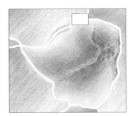

Perhaps the least tamed and, in its own way, most beautiful part of Zimbabwe is the Zambezi Valley below Kariba, ranked as one of Africa's last great wilderness areas and a treasure-house of wildlife. Here the river runs northwards for 70 kilometres (45 miles) – it then turns east to flow across Zambia and Mozambique – its waters slow-moving, its course changing slightly over time to leave behind great quantities of rich alluvial soils, flood plains, channels and broad, shallow pools. Moisture and warmth combine to sustain a lush ground cover of sweet grasses, and mopane, mahogany, sausage, giant ana and other acacia trees. Beyond the riverine terrace, to both north and south, the land rises dramatically to form the Zambezi escarpment.

In the wet season, when water is plentiful everywhere, many of the region's animals remain on the higher ground, but in winter they move down into the valley, drawn by the river and the fine grazing of its reaches. They are at their most prolific at the beginning of the rains: during October and November the area plays host to nearly 12 000 elephants, 16 000 buffalo (which gather on the terraces in herds of up to 2 000), to multitudes of plains zebra, to roan, nyala, impala and other antelope, to countless baboons – and to the inevitable predators. The great concourse of herbivores attracts lions, leopards and cheetahs, wild dogs and hyenas. Crocodiles bask on the sandbanks, hippos wallow, and a myriad woodland and aquatic birds congregate on land and water.

Some 2 200 square kilometres (8 495 square miles) of this fascinating corner of Zimbabwe are occupied by the Mana Pools National Park, which, together with the neighbouring safari areas, has been declared a World Heritage Site. The park authorities maintain camp sites and two pleasant riverside lodges; among the inviting private safari venues is the well-known and award-winning Ruckomechi Camp.

A quartet of Zambezi Valley elephants luxuriate in the riverbank mud (left). Thousands of these gentle heavyweights move down from the hills in the dry months.

83

A group of impala (above) leap their way to safety through the riverine forest. These medium-sized, reddish-fawn antelope are indigenous to the warm savanna regions; the southernmost extremity of their range is the South African bushveld. Only the rams have horns, which are lyre-shaped.

A game-viewing drive (right) sets out from Chikwenya Camp, an inviting private game lodge in the Mana Pools National Park. Chikwenya, which has links with Kariba's Fothergill Island Safari Lodge, was the first photographic safari venue to be established in the Zambezi Valley, and is regarded as one of the pioneering leaders of conservation in Zimbabwe. The magnificent canopy cover seen here is provided by giant ana (or *Acacia albida*) trees, among the largest of the acacia family, growing to a height of about 30 metres (100 feet). Their big, pink-coloured pods are much favoured by game animals, and especially by elephants, who will sometimes rise up on their hind legs to reach the taller branches. Chikwenya itself is set among equally handsome mahogany shade trees.

The Zambezi Valley is sanctuary for southern Africa's largest concentration of elephants (opposite) outside the Hwange National Park. This splendid bull (right) is irritated by the photographer's presence. Though usually tolerant enough of humans, elephants must always be approached with caution: onlookers should not make any unnecceary movement or noise, and be prepared to beat a hasty retreat if warning signs appear – if, that is, the animal turns full on to face the intruder, raises its trunk and flaps its ears. Left: the shade-dappled grassland beckons after a refreshing riverside splash.

A three-day canoe safari (bottom right) en route from Ruckomechi to the eastern boundary of the Mana Pools park. Trailists are backed by a four-wheel-drive vehicle and a support crew that sets up night-camps (tents, and tables for alfresco meals beneath the stars) at the river's edge.

Aquatic vegetation (overleaf) covers an attractive patch of the Zambezi Valley's riverine terrace. Notable among the forest species are sausage trees, whose tubular, fibrous, seed-filled pods can weigh up to 10 kilograms (22 pounds) and are relished by antelope and a number of other animals.

Burchell's zebra (left) graze in the savanna woodlands of Mana Pools. The animal's stripe-pattern tends to vary according to the particular locality; most of southern Africa's zebra have 'shadow' stripes between the hindquarter markings.

Another ever-present resident of the middle Zambezi Valley is the chacma baboon. This one (above) is warning off an intruding and curious warthog. The chacma and the much rarer large yellow variety (*Papio cynocephalus*)

are the only baboon species to be found south of the Zambezi River. Their principal predator is the leopard.

The dung beetle (right), also known as the sacred scarab of Egypt, is a member of the huge (15 000-strong) Scarabaeidae family. The insect is notable for the way it uses its hind legs to roll outsized balls of dung to a chosen place for burial. Once safely beneath the ground, the ball serves as both a sustaining food larder and a nest for the beetle's eggs.

Girded around by a magnificent stand of acacia and mahogany trees on the western boundary of the Mana Pools park is Ruckomechi (below), a riverside venue that has regularly been adjudged Zimbabwe's best safari lodge. The camp, in the remote wilderness flanking the Zambezi, is open only from April to November, which is the dry season, and caters for a maximum of 20 guests in its ten thatched chalets. Each has en-suite facilities; pictured (opposite bottom) is one of the charmingly unpretentious open-air bathrooms. The camp's central complex of bar, dining and lounge area – which comprises a deck overlooking the river – is especially attractive. The resident game guides, well trained and immensely knowledgeable about the ways of the wild in general and those of the river-valley in particular, conduct guests on day-drives and night excursions, bush walks and sunset canoe trips. One of the more prominent birds seen along the river reaches is the long-necked goliath heron (opposite top), the largest of the world's many heron species. Apart from its size – it has a length of about 140 centimetres (55 inches) – it is distinguished by its reddish brown head and neck.

HIGHVELD CITY

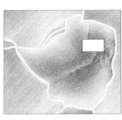

Avenues ablaze with jacarandas and other riotously flowering trees; trim city thoroughfares, clean-lined buildings and the occasional, rather elegant colonial edifice, inviting store windows, animated throngs of shoppers, the whole bathed in the bright African sunshine – these are one's first impressions of central Harare, the attractive capital city of Zimbabwe.

Harare is the base from which many visitors explore the rest of the country – the Victoria Falls and the splendid wildlife sanctuary of Hwange to the northwest, Lake Kariba to the north, the Nyanga and Bvumba uplands along the highway to Mozambique in the east, the grand ruins of Great Zimbabwe to the south, Bulawayo and the magnificent Matobo hills to the southwest. But Harare is more than a mere transit area: city and surrounds have much to offer the leisure-bent visitor.

For local colour, a trip to the vibrant suburb of Mbare is a must: here the sights and sounds – around the vast and crowd-pressed market and the next-door bus station, where upwards of 50 diesel monsters vie for space and custom – are far removed from, though just as appealing as, those of the more sedate uptown area.

Nature-lovers are drawn to the beautiful public gardens, to the trees of the National Botanic Gardens and to the many aloes and cycads of the Ewanrigg reserve. Animals and birds are on view at the Mukuvisi Woodlands and the Larvon Bird Gardens, both on the city's fringes, and, farther out to the west, in the pleasant Lake Chivero recreation area and game reserve. Then there are the famed tobacco auctions, among the biggest and busiest in the world, and, for those interested in the art of Africa, the National Gallery and the Chapungu Sculpture Park. On show at both venues are works created by the internationally acclaimed Shona school of sculptors.

Harare at night (left). Zimbabwe's capital, an attractive city of wide thoroughfares and modestly proportioned but elegant buildings, is home to around one and a half million people.

Harare, founded by Cecil Rhodes's 'Pioneer Column' of settlers a little over a century ago, is a place bright with the colours of flowering trees and plants. Blood-red African flames, crimson poinsettias, bauhinias in pink and purple and white, great tumbles of strident bougainvillea and, most especially, the regiments of lilac-blossomed, springtime jacarandas that line broad avenues (left) bring visual delight to city and suburb. The jacaranda is an exotic species: the first two specimens were brought in from Rio de Janiero by a keen Pretoria gardener in 1888, and have since been extensively planted to grace many a southern African centre. The main flower market (right) flanks Harare's Africa Unity Square (formerly known as Cecil).

The city's main shopping area is First Street (below), whose smart stores and boutiques have been crammed with imported good since controls were relaxed in the early 1990s.

anything you want and much that you don't is on offer in the scores of stalls in the main hall and its surrounds – soapstone carvings, masks, drums, bangles, beads, herbal medicines, trendy T-shirts, eggs, chickens, fruits, vegetables (above), all bargained for and bought to the accompaniment of a hundred blaring radios tuned to heavy-beat afro-music stations.

A market with a different, more measured (but in its own way just as lively) character is the tobacco auction (left). Zimbabwe's golden tobacco crop accounts for nearly a fifth of the country's export earnings, and the Tobacco Sales Floor, in the suburb of Willowvale, is the world's largest – on an average morning 150 million kilograms (330 million pounds) will be auctioned off, rising to 330 kilograms (728 million pounds) in peak season.

Zimbabwe's biggest and noisiest bus terminus and most colourful market-place is Mbare Musika: it's on Harare city's southern fringes and is named after an early chief who is said to have lost his head – literally – in mortal combat with a rival. Practically

Traditional dancers (right) at the Chapungu Kraal and Sculpture Park, one of Harare's major showplaces.

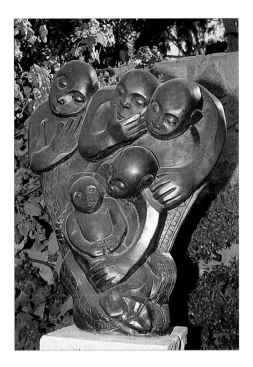

On the eastern edge of Harare is a replica of a 19th-century Shona village where, at weekends, visitors watch traditional African dancing, but which is most notable for the area set aside as the Chapungu Kraal and Sculpture Park. Here, among the rolling lawns, the flowering rockeries and in the indoor venues, you'll find around 200 stone carvings created by 100 of Zimbabwe's finest contemporary sculptors; a dozen other artists and craftsmen work *in situ* while you watch, fashioning powerful subjects from soapstone and serpentine (opposite and left), opal (below), limestone and springstone. Other and perhaps even finer examples can be seen in Harare's attractive National Gallery. The 'Shona school' of modern sculpture, which has been developing since the 1960s, is well represented in travelling and permanent exhibitions from Tokyo to London and New York; each artist has his own, very distinctive style, though there's an impressionistic, intensely spiritual quality common to the best works.

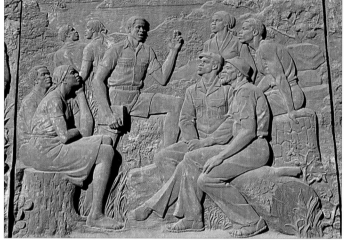

The concrete and glass headquarters of the Standard and Chartered Bank (left), one of Harare's newer and smarter buildings, looks down on the rather graceful Presbyterian church and steeple.

Heroes' Acre, in the woodlands just to the west of the city, is a ceremonial burial ground and monument to the thousands of Zimbabweans who suffered and died during the 14-year bush war fought between the liberation forces and Ian Smith's settler regime. An estimated 25 000 people, many of them non-combatant villagers, lost their lives in the conflict before the country finally advanced to full and free nationhood in 1980. The 57-hectare (140 acres) site's principal feature is a bronze statue of the Unknown Soldier (opposite) that stands on one of the levels leading up to the Eternal Flame and its soaring obelisk. A bas relief (above) depicts scenes from the dark days of the struggle. Other notable Zimbabweans – President Robert Mugabe's late wife Sally, for example – have also found their last resting place in Heroes' Acre.

One of the more striking examples of the 'balancing rocks' (opposite) that can be seen in the pleasant Highveld countryside around Harare.

Anglers try their luck from a canoe on Lake Chivero (right), centrepiece of a recreational park that serves as Harare's main weekend playground. The lake's northern shore hosts yachting and boating clubs, its southern is flanked by a game reserve.

June and July are the best months for viewing the aloes (below) – 57 varieties in all – at the Ewanrigg Botanical Garden 40 kilometres (25 miles) northeast of the city. Rockeries, pathways, trim lawns, a water garden, a profusion of indigenous flora, picnic spots and a myriad colourful birds add to the attractions.

South-central Africa was home to various Stone Age people from about half-a-million years ago, small bands of hunter-gatherers who, over the ages, refined their tool- and weapon-making skills and from whom the San (Bushman) eventually emerged to become the dominant race – and to decorate the caves and granite rock faces of the region with their wonderfully animated art. Most of the paintings are less than a thousand years old; all show the remarkably advanced foreshortening technique associated with the culture – a three-dimensional approach that lends a vibrant quality to the animals, the hunt, the ritual and dance depicted. The colours, too, are strikingly eye-catching, their essence the mineral oxides of the earth: manganese for black, zinc for white, iron for the deep browns, the reds and yellows. There may be as many as 30 000 San rock-art sites within Zimbabwe, including an especially fine one at the Markwe caves (above) near Marondera to the east of Harare.

Quite different in interest and significance are the Chinoyi caves (opposite), carved out of the Hunyani hills 115 kilometres (71 miles) northwest of the city. The complex – in reality a giant sinkhole with several supplementary passages and chambers – is a popular stop-off on the tourist route to Kariba and Mana Pools, its most prominent feature the Sleeping Pool. This 90-metre-deep (300 feet), translucent blue body of water is known in the local dialect as the 'pool of the fallen', a reference to the drowned victims of a predatory Nguni raid in the 1830s. Other sections have equally evocative names, among them Wonder Hole, Sink of Bats and Dark Cave. Visitors can relax in the adjacent and most pleasant park, a shady place of picnic spots and msasa, mukwa, combretum and Cape fig trees.

Some 30 kilometres (20 miles) north of Harare the tarred road comes to an abrupt end at a granite dome, one of many rounded rock formations in an area known as Domboshawa, which also embraces the formidable, granite-cliffed Ngomakarira massif (opposite). Here you'll find caves and shelters that contain some of the finest examples of San (Bushman) rock-art. Domboshawa's best-known site is decorated in a variety of styles and colours; rather special is the 'gallery' of animals grouped around a superb painting of a kudu: wildebeest, a row of curve-horned sable antelope, a zebra rolling on its back, a rhino and an elephant. Humans are also portrayed, most notably in a frieze of animated, 50-centimetre-high (20 inch) figures with very long legs – a representation, perhaps, of the taller Bantu-speaking people who arrived to mingle with and eventually to displace the San. Many of the paintings, though, have suffered severe damage, both from recent vandalism and from the traditional rain-making rituals (ceremonies involve the lighting of fires) of the Shona spirit mediums.

Schoolchildren on an outing in the Domboshawa area (below).

MOUNTAINS OF THE MIST

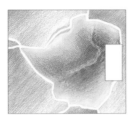

The main highway southeast from Harare to the pretty little city of Mutare runs through flattish countryside for a hundred and more kilometres, until it reaches the small farming centre of Rusape. Then the hills come into view, followed by mountains that sweep up in a grandly imposing series of heights that extend for 300 kilometres (190 miles) along the Zimbabwe border with Mozambique. These are the Eastern Highlands, a land of high massifs and deep ravines, natural forests and vast plantations of pine and wattle, of perennial rivers, crystal-clear upland streams and some of the loveliest waterfalls you'll see anywhere.

The mountains fall into three groups, northernmost of which is the Nyanga range. Here, Zimbabwe's highest peak, the 2 593-metre Inyangani (8 508 feet), towers over the low-lying plain that stretches eastward to the Indian Ocean, and over the fertile Highveld farmlands to the west. Long ago, the region was home to Iron Age communities, industrious folk whose lifestyles are evident in the legacy of walled terraces, forts, stockpens and other stone structures they bequeathed to posterity. To the south of Mutare is the Bvumba range, less formidable than its northern neighbour but scenically just as lovely and famed for its magnificent vistas and floral wealth. Finally, in the far south, are the Chimanimani mountains, different again in their cragginess, in the denseness of their forests and their distinctive plant life.

Much of the Eastern Highlands region is conserved within well-maintained national parks and reserves that offer the visitor a wide variety of attractions – walks through a countryside that delights the eye at every turn; memorable vistas; fishing in the cold, clear, trout-filled mountain streams; golf courses that rank among Zimbabwe's finest, and country inns which are supremely comfortable, and which receive and look after their guests with the kind of old-world hospitality that is rare in the modern world.

The aptly named Bridal Veil waterfall (left) cascades gently into its placid, fern-fringed pool in the Chimanimani mountains.

111

A typical Nyanga countryside scene (opposite); the imposing, granite heights sweep down to grassy slopes, pine plantations and patches of natural forest. Much of the area – 33 000 hectares (81 562 acres) in all – is embraced by the Nyanga National Park which safeguards the forests and the misty heaths; just to the south are the Mutarazi Falls, forming part of the Nyanga National Park. The

Mutarazi cascades, Zimbabwe's highest waterfall and Africa's second highest, plunge down, in two stages, to the Honde Valley 760 metres (2 500 feet) below.

The Ziwa ruins near Nyanga village (right) are the location of a museum whose exhibits provide insight into the ways of the ancients. Iron Age remains – dry-stone walled structures that served as stockades,

fortresses and retaining walls designed to keep the hillside soils in place – are to be seen throughout the Nyanga area. A path leads from Ziwa to the nearby, and especially impressive, Nyahokwe ruin-site.

The Nyanga region is peopled by the Manyika group of the Shona, most of whom make a living from the land, others from roadside stores such as this one (below).

Fly-fishermen (above) come from afar to try their luck, and show their skill, in the cool, clear upland rivers and streams of Nyanga.

A riding party from Troutbeck (left) sets out towards the imposing northwest escarpment of the mountain region. Not too many decades ago the countryside here was bleak moorland, magnificent in its empty vastness but devoid of trees and inhospitable to visitors. Then, in the 1950s, the extremely comfortable Troutbeck resort hotel made its appearance, dense pine forests were planted out on the hillsides, artifical tarns created and a superb nine-hole golf course laid out.

Splendid vistas unfold from the top of World's View (opposite). The vantage point, 2 160 metres (7 087 feet) above sea level, is within comfortable walking distance of Troutbeck Inn.

Crossing the Nyanga area's many highland streams (overleaf). The region is a paradise for hikers.

The emerald-green of the Aberfoyle tea plantations (top) grace the hugely fertile Highlands countryside. Tea-bushes are harvested by pickers wearing wicker back-baskets. Mount Inyangani, the country's highest mountain at 2 593 metres (8 508 feet), backs onto the Aberfoyle plantations and its impressive bulk is more often than not shrouded in mist.

Tea plantations (right) in the Honde Valley form an attractive, as well as an economically important, feature of the Eastern Highlands.

Coffee is a primary crop (left) in Zimbabwe and some of the country's best coffee is grown on the Bvumba's lower slopes. Much of it is exported to overseas markets.

Mutare (opposite), the capital of the Eastern Highlands area, is an attractive city embraced by high mountains, its avenues graced by a profusion of jacaranda, flame and other flowering trees, the main street by stately palms. The surrounding countryside is largely given over to tea and timber, to subtropical fruits, livestock and tobacco (above) on the Highveld to the west.

Zimbabwe's national flower is the lovely *Gloriosa superba*, or flame lily (right), whose long petals vary in colour from pure yellow to blood-red. The plant, a familiar sight in the eastern region, was adopted as a national emblem after a diamond flame-lily brooch was presented to Queen (then Princess) Elizabeth during the Royal visit of 1947.

In the beautiful Imbeza Valley, some 13 kilometres (8 miles) from Mutare, is the Norman-towered La Rochelle, one-time home to British industrial tycoon Sir Stephen Courtauld and his wife. The 14-hectare (35 acre) property (opposite), famed for its exotic trees, ornamental shrubs and rare orchids (left), was bequeathed to the nation and is now administered as a show-place. Its garden incorporates a braille trail, one of only two in southern Africa (the other is at Kirstenbosch, on South Africa's Cape Peninsula).

Hugging the mist-wreathed mountains to the south are the Bvumba Botanical Gardens (below), a 1 560-hectare (3 856-acre) floral sanctuary which encloses a landscaped section of quite magical beauty. Here one can see Zimbabwe's highland plant life in all its variety, together with a wealth of exotic species; pathways, ponds, streams and wooden bridges are girded around by fuchsias, hydrangeas, azaleas and lilies. Nearby is the Bunga Forest Botanical Reserve, haven for a splendid array of indigenous trees.

Hidden among the woodlands of the Bvumba mountains, 38 kilometres (24 miles) south of Mutare, is Leopard Rock (above), an exceptional resort hotel with a rather chequered history. Queen Elizabeth, now the Queen Mother, stayed at the hotel in 1953 and, though the place was something of a visual oddity (it resembled a Scottish moorland castle, complete with towers and battlements), she described it as the most beautiful spot in Africa. Much later, during the tragically destructive bush war, it was damaged by rocket fire, and for some years lay virtually abandoned – until a local tobacco tycoon took it over and transformed it into one of Zimbabwe's finest resort complexes. Among its attractions are landscaped grounds, a superb golf course, croquet lawn, conservatory and casino.

Farther south, beyond the village of Chipinge, is the Chirinda Forest Botanical Reserve (opposite), created to protect one of Zimbabwe's few surviving primeval rain forests. Although the sanctuary is notable principally for its rare, ancient and huge red mahoganies, its fig trees and ironwoods and other handsome species, it is a wholly integrated ecosystem that also sustains many other life forms.

The Chimanimani range is the third and arguably the most scenically dramatic segment of the eastern rampart, a land of lichen-covered cliffs and crags (opposite), of plunging valleys, dense forests, ice-cold mountain streams and waterfalls of breathtaking beauty. Almost the entire highland area is encompassed within the Chimanimani National Park, haven for a wildlife complement that includes the stately sable antelope and the klipspringer, baboons and a myriad smaller creatures, and for a heath-type plant life whose proteas, everlastings and ericas recall the distinctive character of South Africa's famed Cape Floral Kingdom. The park, which is accessible only by foot, is a paradise for hikers, rock scramblers and climbers.

Tessa's Pools (above), one among many entrancing waterfalls in the Chimanimanis. Nearby is the well-sited Outward Bound Adventure School.

The colourful reed frog (*Hyperolius marmoratus*) (left). Breeding colonies fill Chimanimani's night-time air with a sustained symphony of croaks.

LAND OF THE BAOBAB

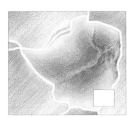

The southeastern segment of Zimbabwe is known as the Lowveld, a bone-dry, ferociously hot region of flattish, dusty plains, stark granite outcrops and ancient, skeletal-branched baobab trees. Over the millennia the soils have been leached of their nutrients, though the scantily grassed countryside does manage to sustain herds of rangy cattle, modest patches of maize, and villagers who have learnt to live with hardship. A harsh land indeed. But parts of this forbidding territory – towards the east, around the charming little village of Chiredzi – have been magically transformed by water drawn from the Lowveld's two major rivers, the Save and the Runde. Great, emerald-green citrus orchards and plantations of sugar cane now stretch to the far horizons.

Farther to the east, occupying the 5 000-square kilometre (193-square mile) corner of the country bounded on two sides by Mozambique and South Africa, is the Gonarezhou National Park, sanctuary for buffalo, giraffe, zebra, kudu, the handsome shaggy-coated nyala antelope, for herds of eland that migrate seasonally across the borders, for hippo and crocodile and for prides of lion. And, especially, for elephants (Gonarezhou means 'place of elephants'), which move to and fro across the national frontiers and which have suffered grievously from the predations of poachers over the years. Nevertheless, their number stands at a healthy 6 000 and more, which is rather more than the park can properly sustain. The park's wildlife tends to be at its most visible along the lower reaches of the Runde River, in the Chipinda Pools area of the park's northern parts, though the somewhat less accessible 2 000-square kilometre (772-square mile) Mabalauta section in the south contains larger concentrations of big game.

Gonarezhou, like every other park in today's Africa, has its problems: years of savage drought, the demands made upon its rivers by extensive irrigation schemes, the ravages of an over-large elephant population, the relentless inroads made by poachers. Potentially, however, it remains one of Africa's finest conservation areas.

A primeval baobab tree (left) is silhouetted against the storm-darkened sky in Gonarezhou National Park. The larger specimens are thought to be nearly 3 000 years old.

The lovely impala lily (opposite top), or Sabi Star (*Adenium multiflorum*) is common in the lower-lying areas of Zimbabwe, its clusters of star-shaped flowers blooming in winter and early spring.

Yellow-billed storks (opposite bottom) cluster on the boulder-strewn bank at Chipinda Pools. These large birds, distinguished by their long

necks and legs and comparatively short tails, nest in trees and on the cliffsides beside open water. They are normally silent except during the breeding season.

A herd of elephants (above) lumbers across the Runde River's dry bed in Gonarezhou. Drought, and the insatiable thirst of the Lowveld's plantations, have led to a

critical shortage of water at times. The Runde, the park's major watercourse, is girded for 32 kilometres (20 miles) by the dramatically sculpted red-sandstone ramparts of the Chilojo Cliffs, seen here in the background. In periods of normal flow the waters are home to tigerfish and bream, to lungfish and, surprisingly, to two marine species: the swordfish and the tarpan.

A giraffe makes its lordly way along the Runde's bank (opposite). The Chilojo Cliffs, a section of which can be seen in the background, are cut through by gullies that game animals follow to get to the water.

The Gonarezhou park is divided into two distinct sections, each with its own network of game-viewing roads (there are no internal connecting routes: the land in between them is untouched wilderness).

The northern area – named Chipinda Pools after its principal feature – is rugged bush terrain suitable only for four-wheel-drive vehicles (above) and internal travel is restricted during the November-April rainy season. Through this wild, game-rich countryside runs the Runde River, its course taking it eastwards to join the Save. At their confluence, close to the Mozambique border, is a broad area of wetland that attracts a

magnificent array of animals and many of the park's 230 species of bird. Chipinda is served by pleasant lodges and camps, one of them set beside a series of spectacular 10-metre (33 feet) cascades known as the Chivirira Falls. The park's southern section, Mabalauta, is flanked by the Mwenezi River, a substantial watercourse which sustains a profusion of wildlife, five caravan-camping sites and the Swimuwini rest-camp.

Two of the Gonarezhou's 6 000 elephants tear at the soft bole of a giant baobab (bottom). The trunks of these grotesque dryland trees can measure nearly 30 metres (100 feet) in circumference; their large, egg-shaped fruits contain tartaric acid and potassium bitartrate (also known as 'cream of tartar') which, when mixed with water, makes a refreshing drink. Animals also relish the fruit. Myths and legends wreathe the baobab: some rural folk believe that God planted it upside down; others that its blossoms are haunted by spirits and that anyone picking them will fall prey to lions.

White rhinos (left) are now a rarity in Gonarezhou. The environment is ideal for this primeval mammal, but poachers have taken a devastating toll of its numbers throughout Zimbabwe.

Buffalo (opposite) congregate around one of the Runde River's few pools of water to have survived the long, harsh winter drought.

The attractive Induna Lodge (overleaf), close to the Gonarezhou park, is one of two private safari lodges on the Lowveld's vast Lone Star ranch.

The countryside to the east of
Masvingo (above) is dry, rocky,
rather bleak, almost unbearably hot
in the summer months, but people
still manage to extract a living from
the unforgiving land. Its greatest
asset is the Save River, which flows
south across the eastern Lowveld
and then joins the Runde to cross
the Mozambique plain before dis-
charging into the Indian Ocean.

The main highway east from
Masvingo and Great Zimbabwe
to the Eastern Highlands crosses
the Save River over the Birchenough
(opposite), a single-arch structure
built in the 1930s and ranked, at
the time, as the world's second
largest suspension bridge. Apart
from its smaller size, it is a precise
replica of Australia's famed Sydney
harbour bridge.

HOUSES OF STONE

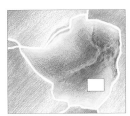

Among the umbrella trees and succulents of the veld a few kilometres south of Masvingo is a vast complex of granite ruins that are ranked as the largest ancient structures south of the Sahara. The walls of the Great Enclosure are 11 metres (36 feet) high, 243 metres (797 feet) in circumference and their million and more pieces of hand-hewn interlocking stones have remained in place over the centuries without the aid of mortar. Within the Great Enclosure is a strange conical tower; the valley below embraces an extensive jumble of lesser ruins; across the valley, atop a cliff, is the Hill Complex, an intricate series of crumbling chambers, stairways and winding passages.

This is Great Zimbabwe, 720 hectares (1 780 acres) in extent, once a bustling city of 40 000 people and the fast-beating heart of the once all-powerful but now long-gone Shona-Karanga empire that stretched from Botswana across the subcontinent to the Indian Ocean.

'Zimbabwe' means 'house of stone', and these splendid ruins are just one (but of course by far the grandest) of some 150 *zimbabwes* scattered across the country. Although the site had been occupied during the early part of the first millenium, the city's three main sections – enclosure, valley and hill – were built between AD 1000 and 1200, and for three centuries thereafter the Karangan kings ruled over much of south-central Africa, their power and prosperity derived from the cattle and crops of a fertile countryside, from the gold and iron of the wider region, and from their trade with far-flung lands.

To the northeast of Great Zimbabwe lies Lake Mutirikwi, a 90-square kilometre reservoir (35-square miles) created to feed the Lowveld's ever-thirsty citrus and sugar cane plantations – and, as a bonus, to function as a pleasant recreation area. The lake is home to hippo, crocodile and a fine array of birds; the adjoining park sustains an impressive variety of game animals.

The view from Great Zimbabwe's Hill Complex (left). A scatter of more modest stone-walled ruins occupies the valley below; in the distance is the Great Enclosure.

At the height of its power Great Zimbabwe was a visual symphony of African architecture and decorative art, and although some of the walls have crumbled and the paint, the moulded plaster, the carvings and other ornamentation are long gone, something of the city's beauty and opulence can be glimpsed in the stonework patterns that still grace several structures (above), among them chevron, dog's-tooth and herringbone motifs.

The valley of Great Zimbabwe contains a profusion of strikingly handsome aloes (right). Few of the materials used by the ancients, either for building purposes or for their advanced craft-work, were acquired in the immediate vicinity. Granite was quarried 25 kilometres (15 miles) from the city; gold and iron brought in from the wider region; copper and cotton (Great Zimabwe supported a thriving textile industry) came from the far north.

Within the Great Enclosure is a cone-shaped tower (left), somewhat reminiscent of a giant grain basket, symbol of abundance and one of the last structures to be built at Great Zimbabwe. On show in the museum is an intriguing array of cultural exhibits, including strikingly original wood carvings (below left).

Over the decades practically everything that was movable from Great Zimbabwe fell prey to looters and to amateur archaeologists. Early in the century an American visitor removed 18 kilograms (40 pounds) of gold artefacts; others followed, among them two Englishmen who unearthed nearly six kilograms (13 pounds) of gold beads from the gravels, and then set up a company which made off with another 14 kilograms (31 pounds). All these relics were melted down; others – notably pieces of pottery – simply disappeared. The treasures inspired European travellers to romantic visions of Ophir and the mines of King Solomon, and of Great Zimbabwe's exotic origins, but the most important of the finds – eight carvings of the famed 'Zimbabwe Bird' (below right) – are, like the entire city, the work of the Shona-Karangans. Fashioned from soapstone and just over 30 centimetres (12 inches) in height, the carved figures are stylized representations of the African fish eagle, sacred to one of the Karanga groups. The bird is now a Zimbabwean national symbol.

Close to Great Zimbabwe, and indeed an integral part of the visitor's tour, is a re-created 19th-century Shona village (left), which provides an intriguing glimpse at a world – an ancient culture – that is fast disappearing. Of particular interest is the resident diviner, or spirit medium (above). Also well worth exploring is the National Museum. A fascinating variety of arte-facts have been unearthed from the ruins: soapstone plates and decorative carvings, iron hoes and an iron gong (both these were symbols of royalty), axes, chisels, copper spearheads and the celebrated Zimbabwe Birds. These are all of local origin. Exotic relics, attesting to a flourishing trading rela-tionship with distant lands, have also been found, among them glass beads (probably from India), some 13th-century Chinese dishes and a gold-and-blue Persian earthenware bowl. Many of the discoveries are on display.

Lake Mutirikwi (right) is the south-central region's premier recreational attraction. The area suffered badly from drought during the 1980s and early 1990s, but in years of good rains the waters sustain hippos, crocodiles, a prolific bird life, large-mouth bass – up to 4 kilograms (9 pounds) in weight – and a wealth of other aquatic creatures. Along the shores are boat clubs, a pleasant rest-camp and camping sites.

The miombo and acacia thorn scrub of the game park that flanks the lake are home to buffalo, giraffe, wildebeest, and an especially impressive variety of antelope, including the largish, rough-coated waterbuck. Male waterbuck have long, forward-curving horns; pictured drinking her fill at a waterhole (top) is a female. Zebra (above) make their way through Lake Mutirikwi Recreational Park's woodlands.

The countryside of Zimbabwe's south-central parts – the so-called 'middleveld' – is distinguished by huge, granite, dome-like formations, this one (opposite) serving as an imposing backcloth to an unpretentious wayside hostelry. Among crops grown in the region are golden sunflowers (below), a valuable source of vegetable oil.

Just outside the town of Masvingo, on the road to Chipinge, is the tiny and strikingly attractive chapel of St Francis, whose walls are entirely covered in what appears to be mosaic but which, in reality, comprises a series of hand-painted murals (right). The ceiling depicts the Nativity scene and the Crucifixian; other frescoes portray St Francis himself; stained-glass windows enhance the decorative charm. The chapel, its shell a modest hut set next to a military camp, is the creation of Italians taken prisoner in the Second World War battlefields of Abyssinia and the Western desert. More than 70 of them died during their years in captivity.

WILDERNESS OF GRANITE

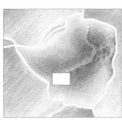

Zimbabwe's second city and capital of the Matabeleland region has curiously impermanent origins, its early history unfolding in three different locations. The first town, 20 kilometres (12.5 miles) south of the present site, functioned in the 1870s as the Ndebele king Lobengula's royal kraal, a huge, enclosed concourse of beehive-shaped dwellings, a citadel named guBuluwayo in commemoration of an especially bloody battle for succession (the word means 'place of slaughter'). Lobengula then moved his headquarters north in search of better grazing land, and in 1893 fought and lost to the invading white colonists. The second guBuluwayo was burnt to the ground, and a new town, colonial rather than African in character, began life on the banks of the Matsheumhlope River.

Bulawayo grew into a busy little metropolis of broad, tree-lined streets, low-rise buildings that were elegant enough in their way, and lovely open spaces greened by the waters of the river. Central Park and its adjoining area is graced by palms and other stately trees, subtropical shrubs and sweeping lawns, an enchanting rose garden, an aviary and game enlosure and, on its boundary, the noted Natural History Museum, repository for an impressive 75 000-piece mammal collection. Among other drawcards in and around the city are the Mzilikazi Art and Craft Centre, which produces, among other things, characterful scultpural work, and the Chipangali haven for injured and abandoned animals.

The most compelling of the wider region's attractions, though, are the ancient ruins of Kame, second in size only to Great Zimbabwe, and the awe-inspiring tumble of granite formations to the south of the city. Here, among the hauntingly beautiful Matobo Hills, the oracles received the words of the Shona-Karanga deity; here the great warrior-king Mzilikazi left his mark and was buried, and here Cecil Rhodes made peace with the Ndebele people at a succession of *indabas* and returned, less than a decade later, for his final rest.

Cecil Rhodes, who died in 1902, asked that he be buried in his beloved Matobo Hills. His body lies among the boulders on the summit of World's View, as does the body of his aide and close friend, Dr Leander Starr Jameson (left).

Three faces of an African city: One of Bulawayo's splendid flamboyant trees (above), or royal poincianas. The species, indigenous to the Indian Ocean island of Madagascar, is rivalled in beauty, perhaps, only by the city's lilac-foliaged jacarandas. Bright paintings of real charm (left) are among much else on offer from street vendors. Bulawayo has a solid industrial base – textiles, tyre manufacture, vehicle assembly, electronic goods, printing, packaging and railway maintenance are among major economic activities – but jobs in the formal sector are hard to find, and unemployment remains high. Outlets for productive talent include the Mzilikazi Art and Craft Centre, launched in 1963 to help disadvantaged women to earn a living turning out earthenware and ceramic pottery; the Bulawayo Home Industries organization (fabric-based crafts) and the long-established Jairos Jiri enterprise (quality African items fashioned by handicappd Bulawayans). The venerable Bulawayo Club (opposite) fronts onto a pleasant, tree-lined thoroughfare. The unusually wide streets were originally designed to enable eight-span ox-wagons to manoeuvre in comfort.

The first train to Zimbabwe (then Rhodesia) puffed its way into Bulawayo on 4 November 1894 on the latest stretch of the projected Cape-to-Cairo route; the city is still the centre of the national railways system. The network extends across 3 394 kilometres (2 109 miles) of track and is largely diesel-driven, though a few grand old workhorses from the age of steam still function at marshalling yards. Others do duty on the tourist runs.

Much of the early story unfolds at Bulawayo's open-air Railway Museum, in the suburb of Raylton. Exhibits include nine vintage locomotives (the earliest is the venerable 'Jack Tar', built in 1896), a museum coach dating to 1904, and the Pullman saloon used to transport the body of Cecil Rhodes to the Matobo Hills in 1902. 'Billy' (opposite) is a giant steam locomotive from the railways' golden middle years. Among other

showpieces are a 1913 travelling crane, and a tin-roofed railway station from the early 1930s; historic engine plates on view include these two (below left). Maintaining the engines is grimy work; pictured (below right) is one of the skilled fitters who keep the old locos on track. Arguably the most inviting of the various steam-train excursions on offer within southern Africa is the five-day safari that begins and ends in Bulawayo,

taking in both the Hwange National Park and the Victoria Falls. Passengers are accommodated in vintage coaches divided into luxurious compartments (some have private lounges); the locos are among the largest ever built; the cuisine is top-of-the-range. At Hwange, there is time to de-train for an extended game-viewing trip, and to overnight at one or other of the area's attractive camps, lodges and hotels.

A short drive to the south of Bulawayo will bring you to the Chipangali Wildlife Orphanage, a haven for sick, hurt and abandoned animals, a few of which are returned to the wild after rehabilitation. The inmates, which number in their hundreds, range from the massive rhino to lion, leopard, cheetah, hyaena, baboon, monkey, aardwolf, serval, caracal, jackal, pangolin, mongoose, vulture, flamingo and python. Attached to the orphanage is a duiker research and breeding centre, which investigates the habits and problems of this small and all-too-vulnerable sub-Saharan antelope.

Visitors explore the orphanage's parkland along shady, aloe-lined pathways that lead past the enclosures – the carnivore section, the python house and so on. Birds of prey have their own flight aviary, aquatic birds their embowered patch of pristine wetland, crocodiles their reed-lined pools.

Many of the animals and birds are 'adopted' by sponsors from various parts of the world (their support is gratefully acknowledged in the lists of names at the interpretive centre and information gallery); Britain's Princess Diana is Chipangali's patron.

At the lion enclosure (above); one of the orphanage's well-trained assistants comforts an infant baboon (left); one of the resident leopards (opposite) – in prime condition, beautiful, and wary of the camera.

In a well-treed and beautiful valley 15 kilometres (9.5 miles) to the west of Bulawayo are the famed Kame ruins, seat of the Torwa dynasty between the 15th and 17th centuries, its community flourishing until Mzilikazi's invading Ndebele occupied it at the end of the 1830s. Thereafter, the citadel was held as a 'royal preserve' – sacred ground and a secret place hidden from prying European eyes – until 1893, when Lobengula, successor to Mzilikazi, fled from advancing settler columns, exposing Kame to the legalized looters of the Rhodesia Ancient Ruins Company.

Massive retaining walls (left) supported earth-filled platforms on which the wealthy and powerful erected their dwellings. Haemotite and graphite were used in the decoration of walls, ornaments and pottery. A draughts-like game called *isafuba* (top and above) was introduced to the Shona-Karanga by Arab traders, and is today still played in many parts of Africa. This 'board' is among the site museum's exhibits.

The moody and magnificent hills of the Matobos (overleaf), seen from the heights of World's View.

The grand Matobo Hills to the south of Bulawayo are noted for their massive and in some instances curiously shaped rock features, many of them of the 'balancing' type (opposite). Matobo in fact means 'bald heads', the name conferred by Mzilikazi in one of his rare moments of whimsy: the great, rounded domes and whalebacks of the area reminded him of an assembly of his elderly counsellors.

Part of the region has been set aside as the Matobo National Park, a 44 000-hectare (108 749 acres) swathe of outcrops and msasa woodland that sustains, among other wildlife, an impressive leopard population and some fine birds of prey, including large numbers of black eagles (below left), which count the common rock lizard (below right) among their prey.

Atop World's View are the graves of both Cecil Rhodes and his lifelong lieutenant Leander Starr Jameson ('Dr Jim'), together with a romanticized frieze (bottom) depicting the last stand of the Shangani Patrol, a settler raiding party wiped out during the 1893 Matabele 'rebellion'.

For centuries the Matobo Hills were both home to and sanctuary for groups of San people, arguably the greatest of all prehistoric artists. Their legacy, rich in both talent and spiritual significance, is still strikingly evident in the many caves and rock shelters of the national park, among them the Nswatugi chamber (opposite), whose paintings of giraffe and kudu are especially noteworthy. Nswatugi also has an interpetive display and there is a site museum at the Pomongwe Cave.

Several inviting private lodges cater for visitors to the Matobos park, among them Camp Amalinda, which is run by a former game ranger. The rustic, imaginatively designed units are built into the hillside rocks; pictured (above) is the lounge and dining area. Altogether, the park has nine public lodges (at Maleme Dam), four caravan-camping grounds and a network of well-maintained gravel roads. One can also explore the area on foot, and on horseback.

Excellent roads (above) provide access to the Matobo National Park, a rugged region of rock massifs, of black eagles and leopards (the area reputedly holds the world's largest concentration of these big cats). In fact the park is sanctuary for more than 50 mammal species, among them giraffe and hyaena, tsessebe and other antelope. About 175 different kinds of bird have been identified here. The wider region's other drawcards include its myriad San rock-art sites, the uniquely decorated Cyrene Mission, and Fort Usher, where Robert Baden-Powell dreamt up his idea of a world-wide Boy Scout Movement.